Magenta combinations relate to the 8th chakra, Soul Star

Violet combinations relate to the crown

Blue combinations relate to throat and communication area.

Turquoise combinations relate to the throat and heart area

Green combinations relate to chest and heart area

Yellow and Gold combinations relate to the Solar Plexus area

Orange combinations relate to navel area and periphery of body

Red combinations relate to the Base Chakra

Pink combinations for love and creativity

Where possible apply combinations around body to include spine.

N.B.
Pink & Magenta combinations have a close energetic association.

The Chakra (or energy centres) run from the 1st at the base of the spine (Red/Pink) through to the 8th above the crown (Magenta).

Any colour applicable to feet.

- Magenta
- Violet
- Blue
- Turquoise
- Green
- Yellow and Gold
- Orange
- Red
- Pink

Mike Booth

Aura-Soma Handbook

© John Michael Booth 2000
Layout: Annette Wagner
Photos: © Ralf Blechschmidt

ISBN 1 901232 03 4

Printed in Germany/Leipzig

CONTENTS Mike Booth • Aura-Soma Handbook

Introduction 5	B20 37	B49 66
	B21 38	
How does that relate	B22 39	The Master Sequence 67
to a consultation? 6	B23 40	B50 73
	B24 41	B51 74
The Subtle Anatomy of	B25 42	B52 75
Man from an	B26 43	B53 76
Aura-Soma Perspective 7	B27 44	B54 77
	B28 45	B55 78
B0 17	B29 46	B56 79
B1 18	B30 47	B57 80
B2 19	B31 48	B58 81
B3 20	B32 49	B59 82
B4 21	B33 50	B60 83
B5 22	B34 51	B61 84
B6 23	B35 52	B62 85
B7 24	B36 53	B63 86
B8 25	B37 54	B64 87
B9 26	B38 55	B65 88
B10 27	B39 56	B66 89
B11 38	B40 57	B67 90
B12 29	B41 58	B68 91
B13 30	B42 59	B69 92
B14 31	B43 60	B70 93
B15 32	B44 61	B71 94
B16 33	B45 62	B72 95
B17 34	B46 63	B73 96
B18 35	B47 64	B74 97
B19 36	B48 65	B75 98

B76	99
B77	100
B78	101
B79	102
B80	103
B81	104
B82	105
B83	106
B84	107
B85	118
B86	119
B87	110
B88	111
B89	112
B90	113
B91	114
B92	115
B93	116
B94	117
B95	118
B96	119
B97	120
B98	121
B99	122
B100	123
Pomanders	125
White	126
Pink	126
Deep Red	126
Red	127
Coral	127
Orange	127
Gold	128
Yellow	128
Olive Green	128
Emerald Green	129
Turquoise	130
Sapphire Blue	130
Royal Blue	131
Violet	131
Deep Magenta	132
Quintessences	133
El Morya	134
Kuthumi	134
Lady Nada	135
Hilarion	135
Serapis Bey	136
The Christ	137
Saint Germain	138
Pallas Athena	138
Orion and Angelica	139
Lady Portia	139
Lao Tsu and Kwan-Yin	140
Sanat Kumara and Lady Venus Kumara	141
Maha Chohan	142
Djwal Khul	142
Holy Grail and Solar Logos	143

INTRODUCTION

What is incredibly exciting to realise is that the Aura-Soma system has the possibility to help the soul to incarnate. It would be true to say that we each come into incarnation with the possibility of growing our soul. To do that, we need to look at our resistances, which are shown in the second bottle we choose. The way we respond to the interpretation of the second bottle can give us a clue of where our resistance lies. When one enters into the Aura-Soma process, when we are able to offer another person a consultation, we have not only the possibility to share the information, but also we have the chance to become "gardeners" in relation to the soul. This is a responsibility we give to the person who has come to the consultation, and also to ourselves; the more we are able to see ourselves in the bottle choices, the more responsibility we have.

One of the first things to remember when giving a consultation is that it is the potential for something to come through you and therefore a possibility for you to grow a little bit. If you are able to hold that idea while you are working, you have the opportunity to make the right space for the person who has come to you. It is important to remember that the person is coming to you to offer something to you, as well as to receive something for themselves. If you are able to remember that they are there to show you something about yourself. If you can remember that in what you are saying, you are already taking a step towards fulfiling what Aura-Soma can be, something that can be active rather than not paid attention to, something that is in the background. If we look at the four bottles we can say "What has this person come to show me about myself", and if we go a little deeper we could also say "What has this person come to show me in relation to another piece in the development of my soul?"

The concept of the soul is that there is a star which lies above us, something that is outside of the physical and it is this that we need to bring into the physical. If we do not understand what the possibilities are, then

How can we work effectively with Aura-Soma as a system?

Above the top of the head is the Soul Star which contains the whole history of who you are, it is outside of time and the lateral nature of that and has information about all the Beings we have been in the past and all the Beings we are yet to be in the future. The task in life is to bring all that which lies in the Soul Star into the physical, to integrate it into our physicality so that we have access to all the understanding of all the Beings we have been in the past and all those we are yet to be. In relation to Aura-Soma, the concept of the Soul Star is fundamental, because it is where we may come to understand the "growing of the soul".

All the Aura-Soma bottles relate to different aspects of our consciousness and physicality and are thus clues to how consciousness moves in relation to those different parts of our physicality. The understanding through the different levels of training is not only that a particular bottle connects X with Y, but that these bottles can connect us to the radiant body, which means bringing the possibilities down from the Soul Star to the physical. It is how, in each life, we have the possibility to contribute to the growth of the Soul, to come to more clarity and understanding and to bring the colour and light into more balance.

How does that relate to a consultation?

It is similar to selling seeds to a gardener. The necessity is to communicate something about planting the seeds the person has already selected. As a consultant, you may be able to see what the seeds reflect and what might come up within the self if the seeds are given the right kind of energy - the right conditions, sunlight, nurturing etc. If one can make that connection and develop that understanding that the four bottles are reflecting the seeds within the self and the possibility of flowers blossoming, then we can come to understand the nature of a consultation in a different way. The consequence is that the person who has come to you will get something of the transmission of what is being said and then there is the opportunity to do something possibly more significant in relation to the growing of the Soul than many other things that one might do.

When we talk about the colours in the system, it is not just about the colour in the bottles. It is about the three energies that come together within the bottles, the energy of the mineral kingdom, the plant kingdom and the world of colour and light. As you tune into these resonant waveforms, the energy that arises from that process transmits itself to the person you are discussing the bottles with - another example of the help and support there is in the unseen worlds for the work we do with Aura-Soma, to bring what is Aura-Soma to another person. The Devas, Masters, Angels and Archangels are all available at this time, offering their support to mankind to help with where humanity is going in the future.

The arrangement with "Upstairs" is that whoever comes in the context of an Aura-Soma consultation is at a crossroads where they are ready to receive something. That person has come with a gift to give you, and part of that is to show you the gift you already have. The more you reveal to them the more they will appreciate what they have been given through what it is you have to say.

This little book is therefore not a substitute for a consultation, but more a brief guide for a consultant to act as a trigger for your own intuition and inner wisdom.

The four bottles are looked upon as firstly, the Soul bottle; second the obstacles and gifts, thirdly the "here and now", and finally the energies that are moving towards us from the future.

If one looks at the bottles in this way, if you are new to the system, then it might give you a clue as to what the essence of each bottle might mean. This is not intended to be a substitute for a consultation, rather a hint as to what the most superficial layers may indicate.

Aura-Soma needs this simple handbook at this point in time and I am very pleased to make it available.

This is just a simple book, rather than an in depth study. As Vicky Wall always said, "the greater guide is within".

It may also be noted that in terms of usage, I have found that the most helpful bottle for the majority of people to work with is their second bottle. Always allow the client to make the final decision in relation to this.

The Equilibrium bottles are the core of the Aura-Soma system, but two other incredibly important parts are the pomanders and quintessences which can simply be selected through colour correspondence to the base fraction of the bottle most preferred in a selection.

I am also including the Subtle Anatomy piece to give those who are interested an opportunity to have a further understanding of the Aura-Soma process.

The Subtle Anatomy of Man from an Aura-Soma Perspective

There are eight basic colours which relate to each of the main energy centres; Red (1), Orange (2), Yellow (3), Green (4), Blue (5), Royal Blue (6), Violet (7) and Magenta (8). We also have the Gold, a very important part of this energy picture, which lies between the second and third energy centres so we call it the two and a half (2½). This is the area which we call the true aura and within which lies the Incarnational Star. This Star is an infinite or brilliant point of light like a diamond at the centre of the Being. It is the consequence of us having been through the process of the Conception Mandala, which we see as a blue sphere with a brilliant yellow pentagram at it's centre. We came to be human beings instead of, for example, an insect or some other creature by recognising the brilliant scintillating yellow light of the pentagram on the soft pale blue background.

Vicky Wall and I independently both had three near death experiences. Common to both of us was a similar understanding of basic subtle anatomy from these experiences. This particular philosophical foundation is based on our mutual personal experience. The blue and the yellow within the Conception Mandala combine to form the pink (the light form of the red). The caring, warmth and awakening of the pink are the basis, the ground upon which we walk. This is the basis of Aura-Soma philosophy.

The True aura is about the size of a walnut existing in the area around the navel. However, if there has been an intense shock, the Incarnational Star moves towards the etheric gap on the left side of the body below the rib cage and above the pelvis. The True aura is an energy picture surrounding the first cell that came into existence at our conception. The sperm met the egg causing an intense energy explosion and the genetic lineage of both the mother and the father fused in the RNA/DNA double helix matrix. During our experience upon the Bardo we observed this energy explosion and we were attracted to its light and energy. This attraction was governed by our Karma or Dharma. We were drawn to the yellow pentagram on the blue background which paved the way for the light of the Incarnational Star which is at the centre of the walnut sized True aura. In seeing our future parents copulating we were attracted predominantly to the energy of either our mother or father depending upon what our own sex will be. The moment of conception, when the sperm meets the egg, is when we connect to our parents' consciousness.Is this all planned, preconceived a long time before? Yes. It is an agreement we have already made with our parents when they too were out of their bodies.

Is the blue and yellow the same for all humanity on the earth? Yes, whatever colour skin; yellow, black, brown, white or red, we still see the same Mandala. The Mandala is not in any way cultural, containing neither creed nor racial characteristics. The Mandala is not the first cell, it is the precursor that leads to the experience of entering into the first cell.
Consciousness independent of physical form, before

entering into the RNA/DNA double helix matrix, first passes through the blue sphere with a brilliant light pentagram within it. That is prior to the physical experience.

It is said "In the beginning there was the Word and from the Word there was Light", this is the way the order of creation goes.

In the beginning we were three in one. Consciousness existed as the Soul Star, the Incarnational Star and the Earth Star, surrounded by an intense field of colour, our Soul Colour (or Soul Ray).

Consciousness saw this image of a yellow pentagram star on a blue back-ground with nothing else in the perceptual field, it was the totality of reality in that moment of experience. There was nothing beyond this, it is what brought us to be human beings.

The Mandala of the yellow pentagram and blue field flashes in front of consciousness at the moment of conception and attracts us. As we pass through the Mandala, it fades into a field of light crystallising in a brilliant point of light or star at its centre. The colour of the Soul ray flashes around this star (the incoming consciousness) and so, at this moment, we become conscious of the colour of our Soul ray. Was the colour of the Soul ray always there, you might ask? Yes, it is what we always were and it is what we always will be until we've completed the journey and the experience of that particular ray.

We are attracted to the Conception Mandala of yellow and blue but as soon as we enter into its light what flashes around us is our Soul colour. This is independent of any other perceptual experience.

What happens next is a second colour flashes in consciousness which is the Personality Ray. So at the centre is the brilliant point of light and beyond that is our Soul Colour. Then the combination of the genetic lineage of our mother and our father and our own colour come together to form the Personality Ray which sits just beyond our Soul Colour.

Consciousness, as a brilliant point of light, experienced all this at the time of the conception explosion. The RNA/DNA double helix matrix is interwoven with this light, it is almost like a photon explosion. As those two forces come together the RNA/DNA spirals merge, like a light field of the cell - an infinite point of light. Around that, as the consciousness enters into it, there is our own Soul Colour and beyond that almost simultaneously the next colour forms like a second layer. All this happens within the formation of what becomes the true aura. It is a memory that will be with us throughout our incarnational experience at a cellular level.

Simultaneously and synchronously as this is taking place there are another two stars that are coming into proximity to that point of infinite light. These stars nurture and sustain the Incarnational Star. They maintain our integrity and individuality. The Soul Star that ends up above our head, (8th Chakra), is the part of us which always was and always will be. The deep magenta is the shadow, before the light, before the beginning. The deep magenta is the void, emptiness like the infinite blackness or that which was before the light was born. The shadow is only the absence of light. The reason that the Soul Star is not part of the Incarnational Star is because we are not coming into this incarnation as fully realised Beings. The reason we have an Earth Star separate from the Incarnational Star is because we do not only incarnate upon the earth. Speculatively, we may have incarnations on other planets, in other Solar or Star systems, each of these has a unique star energy which is part of the destiny of us as a being on that particular planet.

So when we enter into the double helix matrix our individual colours are represented in the first cell. The explosion in the fallopian tube of our mother has a colour which is individual to us. As a consequence of us coming to human birth the combination of this explosion and the light of consciousness within the blue and the yellow creates our individuality and colour. The first ray around that brilliant point of light after the explosion is the Soul's colour, the Soul Ray of this incoming being.

The walnut like True aura represents the energy field of the Incarnational Star. Within the centre of the True aura, (the walnut), lies the Incarnational Star, and within the Incarnational Star, is a hologram. This centre point of the star is the latent potential of all the Beings that we have been and all the Beings that we are yet to be.

This hologram is inactive in the Eighth energy centre until the energy comes down from the Soul Star to activate the Incarnational Star. (See diagram). Then the hologram opens to reveal a six pointed star. From the multiple choice possibilities before we came into incarnation we agreed to do certain things.

The Soul Star opens up at a particular page of the Akashic Chronicle, at the page of the life we are to enter.

As information and energy from the Soul Star circulates downwards to the Incarnational Star, the hologram in the centre begins to expand and instead of being limited within the walnut it begins to appear in the field around the body and we begin to transform into what has been described as a luminous egg.

The Incarnational Star is two fingers' breadth above the navel and two fingers' breadth inside. This is the physiological location of the first cell which is the source of the Incarnational Star. The reason it is sometimes said to be below the navel is because by imagining the energy of the star to be the size of a grapefruit some people find it easier to centre at the bottom of the grapefruit to find their way in, rather than going straight to the Incarnational Star.

In martial arts this also has to do with stability. Centering below the navel, near the base of the grapefruit, is commonplace in Tai Chi or Karate. Visualise the region of the sternum, the rib cage and the pelvis. Think of a whole circle in that area, take the middle of that circle (as the physiology goes) and the memory of the first cell is in that place, two fingers breadth above the navel and two fingers breadth inside. Depending on the attention depth below the navel this determines the centre of gravity within the body. The deeper the centering, the more rooted on the earth.

It is in the moment of the explosion at conception, with our consciousness of who it is that we are as Beings that the Earth Star and the Soul Star expand into being. The Earth Star is our destiny on this planet for this incarnation. It is pre-programmed and prelogged. Unless we become fully conscious, fully realised beings, this pre-programming means that we are going to be at particular places on the Earth, which is part of what we agreed to before we came in. Perhaps we might visit India, Japan, America or Europe. This was logged into our Earth Star before we came into incarnation.

Consider the Earth as a Being who also has her destiny, who is evolving, who is also linked to us and our evolution. We may be here as an act of repayment for times in which we evolved in relation to her because she is now at a critical point of her own evolution. The Earth is a Light Being with an energy field surrounding her. At her centre is a light source, an energy field surrounds that light source, it is called the 'grid' system and has many subtleties within it including the array of Platonic solids. As our Earth Star connects with that grid system it also connects with the centre of the Planetary Being.

The first steps in our evolution, the unfolding of our destiny upon the Earth is to connect with the Earth Star. As a parallel in any growth work or personal consciousness work, the first step is to be grounded. We cannot begin to get off until we are on. The whole relationship with the Earth Star is fundamental to all ethnic people of the world. The sacredness of the Earth, walking beauty on the earth, the conceptual basis of relating to the Earth as a living Being that needs honouring, that needs recognition, is part of our relationship with the Earth Star. Connecting with our Earth Star is the first step in our work upon ourselves.

Let us understand the importance of this perspective. The Earth is a tiny planet, incredibly small in relation to the vastness of space. In comparison, the Earth is much smaller than some of Jupiter's moons. It is tiny. Imagine we are looking at a bit of dust on our trouser or dress, it is less than that size in relation to the wholeness. It is evolving as a being and we have been drawn here in connection with its evolvement.

The Earth's evolvement, its destiny, is to become a star, eventually it will be a little Sun. If we connect with our Earth Star, and fulfil the destiny we agreed to, we are helping her toward her evolution of becoming a Star. The greater our connection with our Earth Star, the more we fulfil our destiny in becoming grounded. We then discover we are in the right place at the right time, we are in synchronicity. The greater our healing of our time-line, our past experiences, the more we fulfil our destiny in relation to the evolution of the Earth. That is the purpose and function of the Earth Star. As it becomes activated and in harmony we have reciprocal maintenance.

As mentioned before, the Soul Star is our individual page of the Akashic Chronicles. I have heard of a place in India where these Chronicles are written on Bhodi leaves and it is an actual part of a vast "library". The Soul Star, from our point of view at this time, is a non-physical reality. It is a star with a hologram of information to do with all the Beings that we have been since the beginning, to all the Beings that we are going to be in the whole of the process until the end. All that information is up there, incredibly precise, every detail of it. The good and the bad bits and all the bits in between are all written down.

The page at which the book is open, the actual detail, is to do with agreements we made with our guides, our teachers and our Masters before we came in. When we begin to fulfil what is on that page, where we have said "Yes, I'll do that", then we begin to get more in touch with our Soul Star.

We have to accept our responsibility in relation to being upon the earth. We have to accept that we have to come into physicality before the process commences. Connecting with our Earth Star attunes us to what we can do here, it enables us to begin to understand the message of the "page" with-in the Soul Star.

The process of being grounded, of getting into the feet, into the Earth Star, is a process of recognising the beauty of the Earth and the quality of the way existence manifests itself upon the Earth. All of that grounded quality of what supports us beneath the Earth Star becomes more and more solid. That brings energy from beneath us, upwards. In other words, attention first has to go downwards. We have to get into our feet, into the Earth, into the solidity, if we do that it is that attention moving downwards which brings energy back upwards. Equally and oppositely as that begins to happen, so energy begins to be filtered down from above. As we begin to get grounded, we begin to get energy moving towards the Incarnational Star, so then our destiny begins to unfold and a little bit of information and energy begins to filter down from our Soul Star. Immediately it hits a little place on the right side of our chest, this place is called the Ananda Khanda. (See diagram). So the second step is our connection with the Soul Star, the magenta. The magenta energy may begin to filter down through the right side of the chest activating the Ananda Khanda, which is in the turquoise area, and then begins to make the journey towards the middle. C G Jung called this 'the process of individuation'. It is a creative process. The movement from the subconscious unconscious, towards the more conscious and collective, happens as a consequence of being grounded, of being upon the Earth, then synchronicity occurs as part of the process of individuation.

We have described this process of individuation as moving from the personal towards the transpersonal. It begins with a strong memory of the Conception Mandala with the five pointed Star and moves towards the six pointed Star which develops as a consequence of becoming grounded with the Earth Star. This activates the Soul Star which, as we will see, slowly begins to open the Emerald of the heart. By becoming more individual we become more closely in touch with the collective. These are turquoise issues but there is something else which is even more incredible about us because between the Ananda Khanda and the Incarnational Star is the Emerald of the heart.

In evolutionary terms the main proportion of humanity is caught within the functions of chakras one, two and three. Nearly all of us are dealing with our survival issues, dependency and co-dependency, and our issues to do with fear and power. The Earth and humanity are at the same stage of evolution where we have the possibility to begin to open and thus activate the emerald of the heart. The emerald is a mirror of the grid system of the Earth. The emerald of the heart is an icosa-dodecahedron. Looked at straight on the icosa-dodecahedron, which is three dimensional, takes on the two-dimensional form of a six sided emerald. The icosa-dodecahedron is a complex platonic solid which mirrors the grid system of the Earth.

In summary, we have got an individual destiny in relation to the Earth. A Soul or Stellar destiny which is not only to do with the Earth but to do with us as a Being from the beginning of time to the end of time. We have also this process of individuation leading us to the icosa-dodecahedron of the Emerald of the heart.

The only way into the Emerald is through the Incarnational Star as a consequence of the process of individuation. We can get into the heart and experience oneness, but the beauty of this experience, of being in the heart space without connecting with the Incarnational Star unfortunately will not last. It will be just a coming and a going, a little "high". If we come through the Incarnational Star in the process of individuation then it is a gradual unfolding. Next, what happens is, we begin to open a window of the heart, with the possibility of finding out why we are here in relation to our service and how we are to serve. At this point, we get in touch with the reconciling force, the third force, continuously balancing the upward and downward yearnings.

The Emerald is a consequence of Lucifer, it is a consequence of the Lord of Light falling to the Earth. The reconciling force is the Christ energy, we could call it the Awakening Force. My preference for the Christ energy, as an Awakening Force, is not because of any historical being, but because it helps us in the understanding of the green/red relationship. As the Earth Star energy begins to be awakened we bring the attention, which is the light, to the red energy of Earth and it begins to turn pink. As the warmth of the pink energy comes up and warms the Incarnational Star, the hologram from its centre begins to expand, the pink energy then begins to open a window of the Emerald, the green of the heart.

The answer to "Why am I here?" "What am I here for?" "What is it that I am to do?" "What is my destiny upon the earth?" lies in the opening of the windows of the Emerald of the heart at a collective level because that is where our evolution is. As we realise why we are here and what we are here for, the more we bring down our destiny in relation to the earth, the more we contribute to the evolution of the earth, the more we can begin to put the Lord of Light back in his rightful position in relation to the Godhead within ourselves. As the Emerald opens, the grid structure of the Earth begins to come into balance.

This is the basis of the Aura-Soma Subtle Anatomy understanding in relation to the eight energy centres and the three stars.

Transcript of a talk given
by Mike Booth in Spring 1998

B0
Spiritual Rescue

Colour: **Royal Blue/Deep Magenta**

Keynotes: Bringing clarity to seeing and feeling in physical life

Where to apply:
Along the entire hairline, around the ears. In acute cases, it can be applied everywhere on the body.

Main points concerning this bottle:
The potential clarity to see into the shadow within oneself with detachment. The faith to be able to overcome all obstacles. The energy to succeed. The trust to get out of the way to allow the warmth and caring to be expressed in the little things of life.

Specialities of this bottle:
In instances of spiritual crisis, this combination may be helpful. Sudden difficulties with the senses may also be aided.

Issues that may need to be addressed:
Illusions and apathy. Difficulties in relation to finding where one is going. No will to succeed. May be holding on to anger from the past, it is still getting in the way now. Does not want to look into the shadow within, maybe does not even believe there is one.

Physical Rescue

Colour: **Blue/Deep Magenta**

Keynotes: Communication with the Being within

Where to apply: Along the entire hairline, around the throat, neck and ears.

Main points concerning this bottle: A person who has peace and trust and endeavours to put their caring and warmth in all that they do. Someone upon whom you could count, who has the ability to listen and to communicate clearly. It's easy just to feel nurtured by being with this person.

Specialities of this bottle: Belongs to the Aura-Soma Chakra Set. Relates to the Crown Chakra and the Third Eye. Physical Rescue is one of the few Equilibrium oils applied locally, it can be applied to any painful area.

Issues that may need to be addressed: Someone who is holding on to the difficulties of the past and has difficulties in letting go. They crave peace but think it's for others; not for themselves. This might be a reflection of a feeling of guilt or unworthiness or it could also be just not believing in themselves.

Peace Bottle

Colour: **Blue/Blue**

Keynotes: Peaceful communications

Where to apply: The hairline, on the neck, and also the lower jaw. Alternatively, the lower line of this band of colour is to the level of the collarbone: apply around the whole throat/neck.

Main points concerning this bottle: Someone who has a real ability to nurture others, who has an immense faith and trust which is easily communicated to others. They have allowed the Higher to come to them or through them; they know they are nurtured from above.

Specialities of this bottle: Belongs to the Aura-Soma Chakra Set. Relates to the Throat Chakra. It may seem strange, but it may help to prevent stretch marks. In this case, apply to the area concerned. With teething babies, apply the combination around the jaw area. (For external use only). Particularly useful at bedtime.

Issues that may need to be addressed: May be difficulties with the father or the mother. This is then reflected in difficulties with the male, female models within themselves. Difficulties in communication. with a lack of attention. An absence of peace and holding on to one's problems; not being able to let go.

Atlantean/ The Heart Bottle

Colour: **Blue/Green**

Keynotes: Nurturing communications of the heart

Where to apply: Across the entire chest area, in a wide band starting at the collarbone, down to the lowest rib and around the back covering the spinal column.

Main points concerning this bottle: Someone who can really express their feelings and is able to communicate them peaceably. A decision maker who has a love of nature. Someone who is in a position to be able to offer new opportunities to others.

Specialities of this bottle: Belongs to the Aura-Soma Chakra Set. This bottle corresponds to the Heart Chakra. May help to establish contact with Atlantean incarnational experience. This bottle can be effective in animal healing, wherever the ailment. Of particular use to people who deal with animals professionally or privately. People with this bottle in the first, third, or fourth position may gain great benefit from (physical) practical work.

Issues that may need to be addressed: Difficulties with the whole of the emotional side of life. Denial of feelings. Difficulties in communicating one's feelings. Difficulties with decisions and making space to do what one needs for oneself. May be difficulties with a lack of nurturing from mother or father.

B4 The Sun Bottle
Sunlight

Colour: **Yellow/Gold**

Keynotes: Knowledge and wisdom, the thinker, the student, the teacher

Where to apply: At Solar Plexus level, in a wide band around the whole circumference of the body.

Main points concerning this bottle: This relates to somebody with a lot of strength and knowledge in the conscious mind with an immense amount of wisdom within the depths of themselves. Somebody who is often in a position of power who has a sense of humour and is able to deal with life in a sunny or happy manner.

Specialities of this bottle: Belongs to the Aura-Soma Chakra Set. Relates to the Solar Plexus Chakra. May be of assistance to establish contact with incarnations in Ancient Egypt.

Issues that may need to be addressed: Somebody who has a lot of fear about the smallest detail in life. Who experiences difficulty in finding the light within but would be able to see it in others.

Sunrise/Sunset

Colour: **Yellow/Red**

Keynotes: The wisdom to use the energies you have wisely

Where to apply: The contents of this bottle relate specifically to the Base Chakra and should, therefore, be applied as low around the trunk as possible - that is, around the entire lower abdomen and also upon the feet and legs.

Main points concerning this bottle: Somebody with the knowledge of how to use the energy that they have wisely in the world. Somebody who has joy and energy to express it. A leader; somebody with a difficult but joyful path in relation to their mission and purpose. A generous soul who offers their qualities freely to others.

Specialities of this bottle: Belongs to the Aura-Soma Chakra Set, relating here to the Base Chakra. Contains similar effects to the Shock Bottle (B26). May help to establish contact with Tibetan and Chinese incarnations. Could possibly indicate abuse, not only when this bottle is in the second, but also when it is in the first, position. Whenever this subject is mentioned, the user needs to be very careful before making an assessment of this type. If abuse actually has taken place, the aim of the working process should never be vengeful or guilt-apportioning. An experienced therapist is always recommended for any work in connection with this subject. Please read in conjunction with B22.

Issues that may need to be addressed: This can be somebody who has attracted difficult situations early in life or who has been subjected to difficult situations. It has been referred to as a bottle which may indicate abuse. See earlier note in "Specialities of this Bottle". It also relates to shocks at an emotional level. May be an over-dominating person even to those they care for most deeply.

Red/Red

The re-energiser and the basic energy of love

Colour:
Keynotes:

B6
The Energy Bottle

Where to apply: Everywhere below the hip area. Where there is a lack of energy; can be especially suitable for application to the soles of the feet.

Main points concerning this bottle: Somebody who has a lot of energy and zest for life. A new beginning can be indicated by this bottle. It's a very powerful bottle and one which can also indicate the energy for awakening and complete detachment in relation to being able to view oneself and others clearly.

Specialities of this bottle: Especially recommended after serious operations or at times of extreme fatigue. Should not be used too late in the afternoon or evening because it can be very energising and could result in sleep difficulties.

Issues that may need to be addressed: This may relate to resentment, frustration and even anger. A need for energy, a lack of vitality. A feeling that the life energy is flowing away into things that are not helpful or useful, and yet, not being able to be in control of that.

B7
Garden of Gethsemene

Colour:	**Yellow/Green**
Keynotes:	The wisdom to trust the process of life

Where to apply: To encompass the heart and Solar Plexus areas, around the circumference of the body.

Main points concerning this bottle: Somebody with the knowledge of how to make the space for themselves. Also, somebody who has an ability to share their knowledge, being able to express themselves in a kind and gentle way. Somebody who is able to create a homely feeling, even though they may be continually on the move.

Specialities of this bottle: The energy in this Equilibrium Bottle is analogous to the situation in the Garden of Gethsemene, where Jesus underwent his final test of faith.

Issues that may need to be addressed: Fears and anxieties that are troubling the person, not being able to make the appropriate decisions in life and to be able to find their direction. It is almost always a test of faith.

B8 Anubis

Colour: **Yellow/Blue**

Keynotes: Wisdom through inner communications

Where to apply: Around the entire trunk - pelvic area.

Main points concerning this bottle: Someone who has a joy for life, who has a lot of knowledge and peace within the depths of themselves. Someone who is looking for the appropriate direction and because of working on the peace that lies within, is able to find that direction and communicate it clearly, joyfully to others.

Specialities of this bottle: May help resolve guilt feelings from previous lives particularly Egypt or the Middle East.

Issues that may need to be addressed: Somebody who has difficulties with nurturing within the depths of themselves and the fears and anxieties that may ensue from that. May also have difficulty with the expression of many deep issues. A lack of joy even when things should be going well.

25

B9

Crystal Cave
Heart Within the Heart

Colour: **Turquoise/Green**

Keynotes: The Transcendental Heart

Where to apply: Across the entire chest area and around the back to include the spinal column.

Main points concerning this bottle: A very creative person who is able to make space for themselves to be creative and do what they need to do, both for themselves and others. Someone who has evolved their feelings and is able to express them clearly, who is able to express easily what lies upon their hearts.

Specialities of this bottle: May establish a connection with pre-civilisation Atlantean incarnations.

Issues that may need to be addressed: This colour combination may indicate repression and guilt creating problems in knowing what one is supposed to do. A person who has not got their priorities sorted out. The experience of jealousy and envy either being in receipt or in feeling these emotions.

Colour: **Green/Green**

Keynotes: A new place and a new space

Go Hug a Tree

Where to apply: Around the entire chest area and forming a band to include the spinal column.

Main points concerning this bottle: Someone with an empathy towards others. Maybe an ecologist or naturalist or one who has a love of nature. This is a decision maker who has an understanding of others and a clear direction. They also have the possibility of seeing a situation from many different angles and also being able to grasp other perspectives presented to them.

Specialities of this bottle: In this combination are "hidden" B2 (Blue/Blue) and B42 (Yellow/Yellow). It may also be useful to read the information given for these Bottles as it also applies to B10.

Issues that may need to be addressed: Someone who is resistant to change. A need to let go of fears. To learn to give before expecting to receive.

B11

A Chain of Flowers / Essene Bottle I

Colour: **Clear/Pink**

Keynotes: Clarity of mind to love the Soul within

Where to apply: Around the hips, the lower abdomen, the lower back to include the spinal column. Can also be applied around the entire trunk and the throat.

Main points concerning this bottle: Someone who has clarity of mind and is able to give love, warmth and caring to others and to themselves. One who shines the light on the love they have within. Unconditional self-acceptance.

Specialities of this bottle: Part of the Aura-Soma New Aeon Child's Set. Functions as a mediator, it can clear the way where other Aura-Soma substances are not yet working. May establish contact with Essene incarnations. May be able to help a woman who is wishing to conceive.

Note: In Aura-Soma, blue and yellow come together to make red. Red with the light shining through it is pink.

Issues that may need to be addressed: Learn to receive love as well as to give love to others. To learn to be humble in self-acceptance. A need to overcome self-doubt.

B12

Peace in the New Aeon

Colour:	**Clear/Blue**
Keynotes:	Shining the light on nurturing, creativity and fruitfulness
Where to apply:	Around the entire neck.
Main points concerning this bottle:	Somebody who has clarity of thought. A creative person. Someone who has nurturing qualities and is able to communicate their feelings to others. Somebody who is able to listen to their feelings and find peace.
Specialities of this bottle:	Part of the Aura-Soma New Aeon Child's Set. Someone who feels inspired and can speak about it as well as about their intuitive insights. Rather, that it is possible for this person to express themselves when they are in an atmosphere of trust. The Clear/Blue shaken together becomes pale blue (Bottle B50) - a more intense form of blue (blue with the light shining through it).
Issues that may need to be addressed:	Somebody who has a lack of peace; who may not allow their tears to flow; difficulty with the masculine side of the "inner" self. Does not respond well to authority.

B13
Change in the New Aeon

Colour: Clear/Green

Keynotes: Enlightenment of the Heart

Where to apply: Around the entire heart area and forming a band around the back to include the spinal column.

Main points concerning this bottle: Somebody who has made the space to find themselves; discover a new beginning and has let go of the past. A crossroads in life which gives clarity to see things in a balanced and harmonious way. Hidden in this bottle are the colours of blue and yellow which helps in communication of all forms of joy and knowledge within.

Specialities of this bottle: Part of the Aura-Soma New Aeon Child's Set. May be of help with rebirthing. This bottle deals with metamorphosis, the transformation of the caterpillar to the butterfly. The combination helps overcome "spiritual materialism". The oil can help to support the process of understanding but progress in these matters always depends on grace from above.

Issues that may need to be addressed: A time to face our circumstances and make decisions on the direction in which to move. Let go of the past; set new goals and plan for the right time to implement them. We may have to face an ending in one form or another. A new beginning is very much a message here.

B14
Wisdom in the New Aeon

Colour: **Clear/Gold**

Keynotes: A butterfly - clarity of thought, New Aeon wisdom

Where to apply: On the entire Solar Plexus area in wide band around the whole circumference of the body.

Main points concerning this bottle: The wisdom and clarity to discover who you really are - the "inner self". To find freedom through using the wisdom you have within. The ability to believe in yourself brings deep happiness.

Specialities of this bottle: Part of the Aura-Soma New Aeon Child's Set. This combination may help to heal wounds and scars from previous incarnations. In children, it may alleviate the fear and anxiety when starting school or taking examinations.

Issues that may need to be addressed: A need to address anxieties, fears or frustrations. Also, deal with any self-doubt. Someone who needs to release their difficult memories and old wounds and so allow the healing process to commence.

B15

Healing in the New Aeon

Colour: **Clear/Violet**

Keynotes: Elevation of the Soul, purified and healing

Where to apply: Along the hairline and around the entire head.

Main points concerning this bottle: Somebody who has clear vision to see who they really are. A healer who has the clarity of mind to allow their gifts to evolve, the clarity illuminates the shadows within. May also help one to connect with one's service.

Specialities of this bottle: Part of the Aura-Soma New Aeon Child's Set. For women in labour, it may ease the intensity of contractions and could help to bring about a more conscious birth experience.

Issues that may need to be addressed: A person who is in need of healing; who also needs to be in control, not only of themselves but also their circumstances. Looking at situations from a purely materialistic perspective.

The Violet Robe

Colour: **Violet/Violet**

Keynotes: Awakening to one's true self and service

Where to apply: Along the entire hairline.

Main points concerning this bottle: Someone who is experiencing change which leads to a new direction. To help to become aware of who you really are, why you are here and what you are for. The search for real peace.

Issues that may need to be addressed: Someone who may have self-destructive tendencies. A need to address hidden anger or a quarrelsome nature. May be confrontational or need to come to terms with grief. Retribution from others. The drive and determination necessary when things are falling apart.

B17

Troubadour1/ Hope

Colour: **Green/Violet**

Keynotes: A new beginning for spirituality

Where to apply: Across the entire chest area in a wide band and around the back covering the spinal column. If problems are of a spiritual or mental variety, also apply along the hairline.

Main points concerning this bottle: Someone who has found space to show their feelings to express themselves. A person with an inspirational creativity. Has found their female intuition within and connection with their spirituality.

Specialities of this bottle: In this bottle, there are many others "hidden" - for example, B20 (Blue/Pink). It may aid in contacting the incarnations between the 12th and 16th centuries, (for example, with the Cathars and Knights Templar). The Troubadours spread their understanding of the truth through drama, dance and song. Often Troubadours were persecuted in those times.

Issues that may need to be addressed: Someone who needs to let go of fear and anxiety. A need for healing following emotional upset especially disappointment related to matters of the heart. Difficulties with self-doubt, stubbornness and not being able to trust one-self or others.

Egyptian Bottle I/ Turning Tide

B18

Colour: **Yellow/Violet**

Keynotes: Spiritual teacher, having the wisdom to find the healing within

Where to apply: In a band across the Solar Plexus area around the whole circumference of the body and the hairline.

Main points concerning this bottle: The yellow and violet are complementary opposites (the material and spiritual aspects). This is someone who has a broad knowledge; who has spirituality and a healing ability within. The knowledge of how to find the appropriate healing for others.

Specialities of this bottle: May be able to establish access to incarnational experience in Ancient Egypt or in relation to moon worship.

Issues that may need to be addressed: Someone who suffers greatly from hidden fear and anxieties; who may let the imagination run wild. May not be able to think clearly. Fears created by internalisation of thought.

Living in the Material World

Colour:	**Red/Purple**
Keynotes:	Regeneration, we renew our bodies when we renew our minds
Where to apply:	Around the entire lower abdomen/lower back area; in mental or spiritual matters, also along the hairline. Not to be used too late in the day as it may be over-energising.
Main points concerning this bottle:	A well-balanced person. Someone with a lot of energy who can see into spiritual matters. One with healing gifts with which to serve and the energy to make it practical.
Specialities of this bottle:	"Hidden" in this bottle is Bottle B6 (Red/Red). Could help with abuse, poltergeist phenomena, releasing other undesired past or present interferences or entities. Might be helpful with extreme tiredness.
Issues that may need to be addressed:	Someone who needs to let go of frustration, resentment and anger to enable them to feel free. The passion within to be used for the good of the self. A person who is over materialistic and represses their spirituality within.

B20

Child Rescue/ Star Child

Colour: **Blue/Pink**

Keynotes: Intuitional love, communication of unconditional love

Where to apply: Anywhere. With teething babies, apply to jaws and around the entire neck. (For external use only!)

Main points concerning this bottle: Someone who has the peace to communicate their caring and love to self and others. A compassionate communicator, who knows love is a great transformer. The balancing of the male/female energies within. Unconditional self-acceptance through nurturing.

Specialities of this bottle: Part of the Aura-Soma New Aeon Child's Set. Especially useful in polarity work and work with the "inner child". This combination contains the warmth and love of a child, with a child's potential for forgiveness.

Issues that may need to be addressed: Someone who may need to resolve difficulties from their childhood. A need to forgive and accept yourself. A need to be more assertive.

B21

New Beginning for Love

Colour: **Green/Pink**

Keynotes: A new space for a new direction

Where to apply: Around the entire heart area.

Main points concerning this bottle: Someone who has space to give love and warmth to others. Allow yourself to trust and you will then find the love you have. A person with a love of nature, who can see many sides of situations.

Specialities of this bottle: This is a variation of Bottle B20 with the addition of yellow in the upper fraction (a knowledge of the inner child).

Issues that may need to be addressed: Someone who needs to accept themselves. May be resistant to change. Has not yet learnt the lessons life has presented. A need to let go of pride and vanity so that you are able to move forward to the new beginning.

B22

Rebirther's Bottle
Awakening

Colour: **Yellow/Pink**

Keynotes: New perspective. Rebirth

Where to apply: In a wide band around the whole circumference of the body within the Solar Plexus area.

Main points concerning this bottle: Someone who has the knowledge to accept who they are without conditions; to love the self unconditionally. To have a new perspective on life.

Specialities of this bottle: In rebirthing it may help the client and the therapist to attune to the process. Also, see the notes on B59 a more intense version.

Issues that may need to be addressed: The need to look for joy and so let go of fear and anxiety which will allow the love to come through. To get to know the complete you so that you can experience true love.

Love and Light

colour: **Rose Pink/Pink**

Keynotes: Wisdom and understanding to find the love within

Where to apply: Around the entire lower abdomen and lower back including the spinal column. During difficult emotional situations, apply around the whole heart area. When there are spiritual and mental problems, apply along the hairline, too.

Main points concerning this bottle: Someone who gives love, warmth and compassion. To accept who you are with love and so find the inspiration and infinite wisdom within. Shed love and light on the darker corners of the mind. An awakening combination.

Issues that may need to be addressed: Feelings of not being loved through fear and suspicion; frustrations of unfulfilled love. Intolerance, domination and determination.

Colour: **Violet/Turquoise**

Keynotes: The Heart's communication of spirit

New Message

Where to apply: Around the heart area and across the back to the spinal column. When there is a problem with speech or communication, apply around the throat.

Main points concerning this bottle: Someone who has warmth and caring in their heart and is able to communicate it to others. Is harmonious and peaceful; heals through service. A spiritual person. The potential to awaken others that they may remember to give love to themselves.

Specialities of this bottle: The contents of this bottle has much to do with the energies of the planet Venus and thus matters concerning emotional life.

Issues that may need to be addressed: Someone who has difficulties with communication or with feelings that are not expressed. May be suspicious or having difficulty in coming to terms with grief.

B25

Convalescence Bottle/Florence Nightingale

Colour: **Purple/Magenta**

Keynotes: A pioneering spirit, a quest for spiritual knowledge

Where to apply: Along the hairline.

Main points concerning this bottle: Someone with a deep caring for others. A person who is a healer with ability to see the whole picture. Has great perseverance and will complete what has been started. Caring expressed through service.

Specialities of this bottle: This combination may be effective in cases of myalgic encephalomyelitis (ME), an illness with symptoms of extreme lethargy and fatigue, as well as headaches and muscle pain.

Issues that may need to be addressed: Someone who suffers great disappointments; who is in need of love for the self. May be convalescing. An impulsive or insensitive person. This may be a situation of compensation in relation to guilt.

B26

Shock Bottle/ Etheric Rescue/ Humpty Dumpty

Colour: **Orange/Orange**

Keynotes: "Get it together again", the shock absorber

Where to apply: This combination needs to be applied in a very specific way - around the entire abdomen; also from the left earlobe to the left shoulder in a small band downward. Then, beginning under the left arm in a wider band, down the whole left side of the trunk to the ankle. When there are thyroid problems, apply around the throat. When muscles are tense, massage on the affected areas, also around the lower abdomen in situations of extreme holding on.

Main points concerning this bottle: Someone who has insight, using it to help them go beyond their own limitations to meet new challenges. A contented and even blissful person.

Specialities of this bottle: Belongs to the Aura-Soma Chakra Set. It relates to the Second Chakra. On the left side of the body is the "etheric gap" where the "true aura" moves in shock situations. The contents of this bottle, if applied as suggested, may help to restore the Aura to its original position. Bottle B26 is the most popular bottle requested from the Aura-Soma range. It can also help animals, particularly after unconsciousness due to shock or anaesthetics. In animals, only apply around the abdomen.

Issues that may need to be addressed: A need to be able to let go of the past and plan for today or the future. For relieving shock. Unresolved shock can lead to growth of indecision. Difficulty with relationships. May be burned by anger and tormented with fear.

B27 Robin Hood

Colour: Red/Green

Keynotes: Infectious enthusiasm for life

Where to apply: Around the entire trunk.

Main points concerning this bottle: A person with perseverance, determination, energy and enthusiasm for life. Someone who is truthful; is able to make the right decisions and has the energy to put feelings into action.

Specialities of this bottle: This combination, if chosen by a woman, may indicate someone who has a problem relating to men. May also indicate a separation or divorce. This combination may help a person to handle their transsexuality (feeling like a woman living in a male body, or vice versa).

Issues that may need to be addressed: Someone who is burdened with responsibilities; has resentments and frustrations. Wants to be in another's space. Very angry but doesn't acknowledge it even to themselves. Not allowing oneself to feel.

B28

Maid Marion
(Robin Hood's consort)

Colour: **Green/Red**

Keynotes: Energy to find one's own space, pioneering

Where to apply: Around the entire trunk.

Main points concerning this bottle: Someone who has found the space to channel their energy. Someone who is able to trust their intuition. Being true to yourself and others brings more joy and happiness.

Specialities of this bottle: If a man chooses this bottle, it may indicate a problem with women. If chosen by a woman, it may indicate that she has allowed herself to be treated as a "doormat".

Issues that may need to be addressed: Someone not trusting their own judgement because of misplaced trust in others. A lack of confidence as a result of not making space to recognise what is true for oneself.

Get Up and Go

Colour: **Red/Blue**

Keynotes: Right activity will lead to harmony and peace

Where to apply: Around the entire trunk.

Main points concerning this bottle: A successful person, even a materialistic person. Someone who has a lot of energy for life and communicates this to the world. One's survival issues are tempered by the peace within.

Specialities of this bottle: Helpful when one feels low energy.

Issues that may need to be addressed: A need to find the peace that lies within which is overshadowed by the anger, frustration, resentment and the material side of life.

Bringing Heaven to Earth

Colour: **Blue/Red**

Keynotes: Heaven on earth, life's quality

Where to apply: Around the entire trunk. When there are spiritual problems and headaches, apply along the hairline, too.

Main points concerning this bottle: The energy to awaken to who you are and the communication to bring that forth. The peace to be able to examine survival issues. A potential for service to others. A person with inner strength to see things through.

Specialities of this bottle: "Hidden" in this bottle is B20 (Blue/Pink) Star Child. (The intense form of Blue/Red).

Issues that may need to be addressed: The release of anger and frustration. May be a need to heal the child within. There is a lack of communication of the feelings of passion which may be locked inside.

B31
The Fountain

Colour: Green/Gold

Keynotes: Knowing, through finding your own space

Where to apply: In a band between the heart and the area below the navel around the circumference of the body.

Main points concerning this bottle: The wisdom within has found the space to be expressed through the heart giving us joy. Balance - the truth of the heart and the wisdom of the belly. Harmony. An honest person with integrity.

Specialities of this bottle: Can help us to find a personal power spot, a place in nature, where we feel content and especially "connected". Is supportive and maybe calming in facing examination situations.

Issues that may need to be addressed: Someone who cannot express their fears causing them difficulties in decision making. Jealousy, anxiety and envy can prevent one from feeling the positive emotions and energy from the heart.

B32

Sophia

Colour: **Royal Blue/Gold**

Keynotes: A message of good things to come

Where to apply: Around the circumference of the body anywhere between head and navel.

Main points concerning this bottle: Someone who has a well of wisdom within and is able to communicate it for the benefit of others. A person who learns from experience and thus gains wisdom.

Specialities of this bottle: Helps access ancient memory. This bottle may connect with Aztec, Mayan and Toltec incarnations. It is possible that somebody who chooses this as the first bottle was born with the umbilical cord around the neck. (This may also relate to past life experience).

Issues that may need to be addressed: The fears and anxieties that someone holds within leads to difficulties in communication. Can suffer from bitterness disillusionment and intense jealousy.

Dolphin
Peace with a Purpose

Colour: **Royal Blue/Turquoise**

Keynotes: Inner tuition, the communication of the heart

Where to apply: Around the neck and jaw area, along the hairline, just above the eyebrows, the forehead, and around the throat. Also, in a band across the entire chest and back including the spine. With eye conditions, apply near the eye sockets (only upon the bone structure around the eye).

Main points concerning this bottle: Someone who has inspiration and communicates this with feeling to everyone. A calm and peaceful soul who finds being creative a pleasure.

Specialities of this bottle: May establish contact with incarnations in Lemuria and Atlantis. Maybe helpful in polarity work.

Issues that may need to be addressed: Difficulties with authority especially with male/father model. May find that they habitually play the role of a martyr.

Colour: **Pink/Turquoise**

Keynotes: Access to the hidden mysteries of life and love

B34
Birth of Venus

Where to apply: Around the heart and across the back to include the spinal column. With menstrual problems, around the lower abdomen and lower back. In dream work, along the entire hairline of the head.

Main points concerning this bottle: Someone wishing to improve their circumstances. To love yourself and so be able to communicate what is hidden in the heart. The giving and receiving of love produces change.

Specialities of this bottle: Maybe helpful with dream work and for children who feel threatened. Choosing this bottle may indicate that the person could be influenced by flattery and even manipulated by this.

Issues that may need to be addressed: A need to deal properly with disappointments and so help the mind and body heal. To let go of past problems to find joy.

Kindness

Colour:	**Pink/Violet**
Keynotes:	Service with unconditional love, love from above

Where to apply:	Anywhere.
Main points concerning this bottle:	Someone whose spirituality brings them love, caring and warmth to give to others. A self-confident person with the gift of healing.
Specialities of this bottle:	Maybe helpful in situations in which someone suffers physically - for example, if one is in pain, but no specific reason can be found.
Issues that may need to be addressed:	Someone who may be suffering from depression. A person who can be dominated by others or by themselves because of spiritual pride.

B36

Charity

Colour: **Violet/Pink**

Keynotes: Kindness in service, compassionate and understanding

Where to apply: Everywhere.

Main points concerning this bottle: Someone who is compassionate, understanding and has the gift of healing. Time to let go of the past and let the potential for new beginnings expand. Put the energy within into new interests projects and inspirations.

Specialities of this bottle: Maybe helpful when working with our "inner child".

Issues that may need to be addressed: Feelings of not being loved. Someone who worries too much especially in relation to survival issues. May be a person who thinks too much and doesn't allow their feelings to communicate themselves from their heart.

B37

The Guardian Angel Comes to Earth

Colour: **Violet/Blue**

Keynotes: Nurturing and protecting balanced communications

Where to apply: Along the entire hairline and around the throat/neck area.

Main points concerning this bottle: Someone who is peaceful, who has healing ability and is a good communicator. A harmonious person within themselves.

Specialities of this bottle: Can balance and stimulate the Third Eye, as well as help develop psychic abilities.

Issues that may need to be addressed: May think they have no inspiration or intuition. Open up to the unexpected that something new may come.

B38

I. Troubadour
II. Discernment

Colour: Violet/Green

Keynotes: Balance of the conscious and subconscious mind

Where to apply: The entire hairline, around the heart and across the back to include the spinal column; when there's bladder and kidney problems, around the abdomen; also wherever the pain is.

Main points concerning this bottle: Someone who has a balance between their conscious and subconscious mind. An intuitive, spiritual, sensitive person, someone with compassion who brings healing to others. The maternal/nurturing/feminine quality within.

Specialities of this bottle: In this bottle there are many colour combinations "hidden" within. This combination may help to establish access to medieval incarnational experience (see 'Specialities of this Bottle' B17).

Issues that may need to be addressed: Feelings of jealousy and envy. May have a lack of trust through emotional hurts. Someone who is disillusioned, in particular, with relationship.

B39

Egyptian Bottle II
The Puppeteer

Colour: **Violet/Gold**

Keynotes: Knowledge and service, compassionate and understanding

Where to apply: Along the entire hairline; around the abdomen and back to include the spinal column.

Main points concerning this bottle: Someone who is able to heal and is in tune with their own process. An emotional, intuitive person who may be experiencing an inner transformation.

Specialities of this bottle: May establish access to incarnational experiences in Ancient Egypt.

Issues that may need to be addressed: Holding on to anxiety and fear from the past. Self-praise could lead to difficulties in making friends.

"I Am"

Colour: **Red/Gold**
Keynotes: Energy to find self-knowledge, expansive activity

Where to apply: Around the circumference of the body between the Base and Solar Plexus Chakras

Main points concerning this bottle: A person with a positive energy who is in touch with themselves in a centered way. They have the detachment necessary to allow the wisdom within to express itself through them.

Issues that may need to be addressed: Someone who may have anxiety; may also experience other negative emotions like anger, resentment and frustration. May suffer self-criticism and be fearful or anxious. A person who may be manipulated by their own insecurity.

B41

Wisdom Bottle
El d'Orado

Colour: **Gold/Gold**

Keynotes: The cup runneth over, quintessence of wisdom on all levels

Where to apply: Across the entire Solar Plexus area, around the back to include the spinal column.

Main points concerning this bottle: Someone who has joy and wisdom through positive thinking, positive expression and positive action. Has found their pot of gold at the end of the rainbow, connected with their centre.

Specialities of this bottle: May dissolve blockages in the middle section of the body. May help assimilation.

Issues that may need to be addressed: Difficulties with the blockages in the Solar Plexus area. May be withdrawn resulting in fear and anxiety or confusion. Not breathing deep enough.

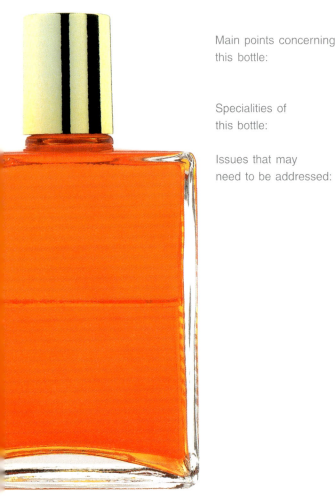

B42
Harvest

Colour: **Yellow/Yellow**

Keynotes: Joy, wisdom, happiness, bliss, awakening

Where to apply: Around the circumference of the body in the Solar Plexus area particularly when experiencing (S.A.D.) seasonal depression (usually in the winter).

Main points concerning this bottle: Someone who has found emotional happiness leading to joy and fulfilment. A person who is aware of self and found knowledge that is able to stimulate their mind. An intellectual who emits contentment.

Specialities of this bottle: Useful prior to examinations. This combination can affect the astral body, it can help us to let go of our illusions.

Issues that may need to be addressed: A person who may have negative feelings or be self-conscious. Someone who is anxious about over-eating or is confused but who is always trying to put on a happy face.

Creativity

Colour: **Turquoise/Turquoise**

Keynotes: Communications of the heart, rely on your Soul

Where to apply: Around the chest box and across the back to include the spinal column.

Main points concerning this bottle: Someone who is able to communicate from the heart in a peaceful way. A person with wisdom within who may be a mystical seeker of unknown mysteries. Creative in all senses.

Specialities of this bottle: This bottle relates especially to the Ananda-Khanda centre, the minor Chakra on the right side of the body at the heart level (just above the right nipple).

Issues that may need to be addressed: A need to acknowledge the fears within. Confusion may be stopping the flow of creativity or preventing them from knowing what it is they want to do to fulfil their purpose.

(Pale Violet) Lilac/Pale Blue

The lilac flame of transmutation, blue of absolute protection

Colour:
Keynotes:

B44
The Guardian Angel

Where to apply: Around the throat and along the hairline.

Main points concerning this bottle: Someone who has inspiration within their heart and the trust to bring it through into reality. Peaceful change. Discovering your own Divinity, be true to yourself, the angel that you are.

Specialities of this bottle: Gives strength to those people who may have had encounters with UFOs, extra-terrestrials or angels, and who, as a result, feel threatened confused or insecure. Everything that applies to B37 also applies to this Bottle in a more intense form.

Issues that may need to be addressed: Someone who is unable to express the feelings in the mind. A need to stop living in the past. May be suffering from illusion or self-deception. Wants things to be a certain way but doesn't know what to do to achieve their goals.

Breath of Love

Colour:
Turquoise/Magenta

Keynotes: The need and the gift to have and to give love

Where to apply: Everywhere. When there is deep stress, apply especially around the heart.

Main points concerning this bottle: Someone who has loving kindness and compassion within that needs to be shared with others. Creative expression - music, dance, poetry - helps with healing the world over. Love - to have and to give through the little things. Brings us in touch with the process of Individuation.

Specialities of this bottle: Assists us to overcome our disappointments in love. To restore creative flow.

Issues that may need to be addressed: Someone who tends to take on other people's problems. A need to allow new love to enter and to let go of past memories that may be stifling happiness. The need to overcome pride.

Colour: **Green/Magenta**

Keynotes: Discovery of inner strength and love

The Wanderer

Where to apply: Around the heart and across the back to include the spinal column; with menstrual problems, also around the lower abdomen.

Main points concerning this bottle: Main points concerning this bottle: Someone who has faith and trust, Divine love and creative power. A compassionate and loving person.

Issues that may need to be addressed: Feelings of jealousy or envy. Someone who has become disillusioned or who will not look at those things which rule their life and affirm patterns that could be let go of.

B47
Old Soul

Colour: **Royal Blue/Lemon**
Keynotes: A time to formulate new goals

Where to apply: Around the circumference of the body in the Solar Plexus and heart areas, as well as along the hairline.

Main points concerning this bottle: Find clarity in the intellect and knowledge within the self. An opening to heavenly peace and inspirational creativity. A person with mystical knowledge and access to the Higher mind.

Specialities of this bottle: The only bottle within the range of Equilibrium that contains the lemon yellow. It has a quality that expresses something coming from another level. Please note that it shakes together as the Emerald Green. It is concerned with connecting with one's deeper purpose.

Issues that may need to be addressed: Boredom over intellectualisation. Hidden fears. Depression due to too much internalisation.

B48
Wings of Healing

Colour: **Violet/Clear**

Keynotes: Spiritual cleanser, a time to look within

Where to apply: Along the hairline; for hormonal related back problems, also apply around the abdomen.

Main points concerning this bottle: There is the potential of finding one's spirituality as the Light shines from deep within. An orator who is fulfilling a healing service in the world.

Specialities of this bottle: This combination is especially recommended after craniosacral work to stabilise the bodies.

Issues that may need to be addressed: The need to clear the channels by shedding repressed tears to be able to find peace and healing.

New Messenger

Colour: **Turquoise/Violet**

Keynotes: Elasticity of the mind through inner communications

Where to apply: Around the circumference of the body over the chest area and along the hairline; with speech problems, also around the throat/neck.

Main points concerning this bottle: Someone with hidden healing qualities which are shared with love from the heart. They express peace and harmony through which they bring joy and happiness to others. Sensitivity in communications.

Specialities of this bottle: May be helpful when there are difficulties with communication. Healing situation where creativity has been stifled.

Issues that may need to be addressed: A need to heal the heart and find love. A letting go of guilt to help when one has lost one's way upon their path.

The Master Sequence

The Master Sequence

The sequence we are going to look at in relation to colour is what we in Aura-Soma call the Master Sequence. These are the bottles which were revealed in the system between B50 to B64. I would like to give an introduction about the way I see the Master sequence and the broader concept. Then I hope insights about colour in relation to this Master sequence will bring a deeper understanding. Over the last two years when teaching Healing Intensive's or the Breath of Life course, whilst using the Quintessences, I have discussed what the Masters really represent and their significance as far as we are concerned within Aura-Soma.

The image I would like to offer you is that of a horse and carriage. This is a traditional image in relation to the understanding of the Master and its position in relation to ourselves. The carriage has two doors, four wheels and a driver that sits on top. Inside is a person being taken from one place to another. The horse is pulling the carriage and has a direct mechanical connection to the carriage. Also, from the horse's mouth there is a connection to the driver, these are the reins which the driver holds to guide the horse. What should we understand by this image?

The horse represents the emotional body. In the West on this planet, at this point in time, the emotional body does not receive much education. From the age of four to six years old the horse is being educated. Even during this period, because most of the horse's education is impoverished, many of the models we have for our emotional body are negative. Little of the emotional food for the horse is of a positive nature.

The higher emotions are aspects that most of us haven't really experienced in our early childhood, the consequence being that most of us are pulled along by an immature, under-educated horse.

The driver represents the intellect. In Western society and actually around the world the driver is over-educated with most of the emphasis being above the shoulders. We tend to think that the mind exists above the shoulders and that the brain that exists in the head is the only source of our thinking and being. Most of the conditioning and education we receive from beginning school through to college or university tends to be directed towards the head and the understanding that is related to the mental body, the intellect. Therefore the driver is over-educated. He doesn't know really what to do with much of his information. It's there but he hasn't connected it with the rest of his being, so it's disconnected, particularly from the carriage which is symbolic of the physical body.

Although the driver is sitting on the carriage the relationship between the two tends to be divorced, resulting in the main responses to the world, to phenomena both internal and external, being purely from this mental aspect.

So we have an under-educated horse and an over-educated driver, connected to each other by reins. Consider then, that if the driver doesn't know where he's going, and the horse is under-educated, then it will be difficult for the driver to control the horse because the horse doesn't understand what the driver really wants. Equally, the driver is not able to clearly express his wishes because he is not fully in touch with the horse. Although the driver and the horse are connected together by the reins, that linkage may not necessarily be effective because the thinking and feeling aspects of ourselves are not well connected (the reins being too limp or too tight).

The horse also has a mechanical connection to the carriage. This represents a direct connection between the horse, the feeling or emotional body, and the whole of the way we are in our physicality. The four wheels could represent the four elements of the physical base, or they could represent other aspects through which we touch the world, namely our sense doors. The condition of the carriage is an expression of how we look after our physicality. Some carriages have nice painted exteriors, some are a bit shabby, some are in different states of disrepair. There are certain disciplines we can do that will effect our physicality to give it the condition we would want it to be in the world, such as exercise and breathing for example. It depends how much attention, in relation to our conditioning, we give to the carriage and its general condition, rather than being the result of the integration of the driver and the horse with the carriage.

The possibility exists within the image that the three aspects can begin to co-operate. The driver may begin to be less focused above the shoulders and more in touch with the horse. The horse can become educated in a different way and be more responsive to the instructions that are now coming from a different place within the driver. The carriage begins to understand, it becomes more alert, awakens and begins to function better in each of its seven energy centres.

What about the person who is sitting inside the carriage? This is really the Master. The Master is always there whether we recognise him or her or not. He or she is sitting inside the carriage waiting for us to give him or her a little bit of attention. Until that point, he or she is an impassive, impartial observer of what takes place in our life. He or she is not in a position of judgement, he cannot do very much, just sit quietly watching whatever takes place. If we begin to give attention to the driver or the horse or direct some of what the carriage is doing towards him or her then there is a considerable shift. He or she is the person who sits silently inside waiting for attention, waiting for a response, waiting for love, waiting for caring at a deep level of our self. If we begin to feed the Master there's an initial and beneficial response in the different aspects of ourselves within our physicality, within the driver and within the horse, immediately there's a synchronicity between all three as soon as the Master is contacted.

How do we get to that place inside to find out where the Master is going? He's the one who knows where the carriage should be heading. He has the instructions regarding the direction of the carriage; the unfolding of our destiny and progression of our timeline. He knows how it is possible for our potential which came into incarnation to really express itself in the world. The driver doesn't know and neither does the horse, but both are an essential part of the expression of what that Master could become in the world, as is the carriage because the carriage is the vehicle through which that expression may take place.

What can Aura-Soma offer to this understanding of the horse, the driver, the carriage and the relationship with the Master? We can say that each Master has a particular colour coat on. Each of us represents a different facet of the diamond, a different facet of the light that's linked to our purpose, our mission of why and what we are here for. You can call these rays or colours or different facets of the light, but each of us has a Master sitting somewhere deep within ourselves that has a particular facet which is a reflection of the one pure light. Aura-Soma, the Master Quintessences and the Equilibrium Bottles that represent the Masters, are pointing in the direction of the horizontal aspect of the vertical transmission that these Master vibrations carry. In other words, they expand in space the possibility for that Master to be heard as a still small voice within. Each of us has that possibility. If we can come to quietness in the mind, then maybe we can begin to hear that still small voice within. By "mind" I don't mean intellect; I mean the whole correlation of the mind/body continuum. If there is stillness or quietness within, the still small voice can have the space to appear. We can invoke the qualities of the masters we use within to express themselves in our life

The function of the Equilibrium Bottles and Quintessences relating to the Masters is to help us as a tool, as a part of the process, to get in touch with what might be the function of that Master who sits quietly inside. As we look at colour, as we look at the light reflected to ourselves, then we recognise the colour of his clothes, we recognise that which lies at the deeper levels of ourselves. The smells and energies help with this process. This is the overall or basis of understanding, the broader picture, and what their significance is in relation to Aura-Soma. The whole system is a reflection of colour and light. We say, in Aura-Soma ,"You Are The Colours You Choose, these reflect your Being's needs". The Being's needs, ultimately, are in relation to why and what we are here for and what it is we are to do. The unfolding of the Karma is what it is that we are mostly about. The seeds we planted in the past are going to have consequences on the life we're in now, until we come to the point that we're in touch with the Master vibration. That is when we step from what's called Karma, planting the seeds of the past in terms of good or bad, right or wrong; to being able to unfold why it is that we're here which is (the path of) Dharma.

Dharma is the way, the unfolding of the destiny. This is when the Master begins to manifest in the life, which is the manifestation of the witness. By the witness becoming more active we begin to watch ourselves from the point of loving compassion, from the point of caring, from warmth, not from judgement. When we start to watch ourselves like a parent lovingly watches a child it is the beginning of the Master energy appearing. We begin to establish watchful alertness, an awareness of being with ourselves in appropriate ways, able to see what we are doing and notice some of our strategies. We watch the way in which we approach things, particularly where its difficult to see what we are doing as we are doing things in relation to the first three bottom chakras - survival issues, issues of dependency and co-dependency and issues relating to fear and power. These are the three centres where we are likely to be fully identified. As we begin to move towards the fourth we begin to access what is inside the carriage. It's not until we begin to get the caring, the warmth and compassion towards what we see on the stage of ourselves, that we can begin to make that movement towards what's going on inside the carriage. We begin to be able to witness what's happening with ourselves a little more, particularly in relation to strategy.

In the Master Sequence we begin to see revealed a

particular order of unfolding and its relation to the understanding of Aura-Soma.

Colour:
Keynotes:

Pale Blue/Pale Blue
The power behind the throne of consciousness

El Morya

Where to apply: Around the throat and neck.

Main points concerning this bottle: Someone who has peace and has found inner tranquillity A person who puts the concerns of others before their own, a selfless person. Peace and communication in relation to the Higher Will. A clear mind.

Specialities of this bottle: The first bottle in the Aura-Soma Master Sequence. Please note, everything that applies to B2 also applies to this bottle in a more intense form.

Issues that may need to be addressed: A need to find balance between either loving too much or not enough in relationship. Depression due to feeling unwanted or unloved. Difficulties in the expression of feelings - the need to get in touch with care and compassion within.

B51

Kuthumi

Colour:	**Pale Yellow/Pale Yellow**
Keynotes:	Two way communication - Above and Below

Where to apply: In a band around the Solar Plexus area of the body.

Main points concerning this bottle: Someone who is seeking knowledge; who has mental flexibility, discrimination, clarity and so is open-minded. Someone who fights for the rights of others; seeker of justice for others.

Specialities of this bottle: The second bottle in the Aura-Soma Master Sequence. May help with the perception of Devas and Angels, as well as communication with them; the awareness of the entire mineral and plant realms and the Beings that occupy these realms. Two way communication - Above and Below. Everything that applies to B42 also applies to this bottle in a more intense form.

Issues that may need to be addressed: A need to be more detached and to let go of anxiety and fear. Not to get involved in disputes or be intolerant of others through one's own fear.

B52
Lady Nada

Colour: Pale Pink/Pale Pink

Keynotes: Spiritual growth through the ability to love, "in the pink"

Where to apply: Around the circumference of the body in the abdominal area. With mental problems, apply one drop to the top of the head, one drop to the temples, and one drop to the back of the neck, and rub in gently.

Main points concerning this bottle: A perceptive and intuitive person. Someone who is able to give the love they have within to others as well as to themselves. To grow spiritually through love.

Specialities of this bottle: The third bottle in the Aura-Soma Master Sequence. In past-life therapy, it may establish contact with Essene incarnations. This combination relates also to the Third Eye and to music, it can intensify the experience and understanding of music. Everything that applies to B6 also applies to this bottle in a more intense form.

Issues that may need to be addressed: Someone who may have spiteful, critical, suspicious or even jealous tendencies. May be open to emotional blackmail. A person, through the holding of anger, resentment and frustration in an intense form, may be empty of love. Not being able to stand back and observe; or not being able to let go and so becomes re-active, rather than being able to be active in situations.

B53
Hilarion

Colour: **Pale Green/Pale Green**

Keynotes: The pure heart, regeneration

Where to apply:	Around the entire heart area including the back and spinal column.
Main points concerning this bottle:	The potential of making space for oneself, for finding the right place. A truthful person. Someone who is able to let go, leaving the past behind and moving on to discover what lies ahead; the way, the truth and the Light.
Specialities of this bottle:	The fourth bottle in the Aura-Soma Master Sequence. May establish contact with Lemurian incarnations. This bottle is often chosen by people who work with body therapies such a Rolfing, Trager, Alexander Technique or Feldenkrais. Any techniques which increase a sense of spaciousness within the body. Everything that applies to B10 also applies to this bottle in a more intense form.
Issues that may need to be addressed:	There may be a need to work on the feelings of frustration; holding on to confusion, separation or deceit. The person may like arguing and relishes conflict. An impetuous person who is in a continual state of anticipation, which prevents them from being in the present.

Colour: **Clear/Clear**

Keynotes: The power of the light, expansive consciousness

Serapis Bey

Where to apply: Everywhere.

Main points concerning this bottle: Someone who understands suffering and is growing within themselves through this. Awareness of the revelations that come from Above.

Specialities of this bottle: The fifth bottle in the Aura-Soma Master Sequence. Serapis Bey can help us to find the colours that relate closest to our Soul ray. Vicky Wall said that this can be one of the more powerful bottles within the whole range. May also be helpful when other combinations are not working as intended, to help stimulate the Aura-Soma process.

Issues that may need to be addressed: Someone who has suffered and could be in great pain. A need to look at one's true colours and cease hiding from who you are ("white with rage"). A domineering person.

B55
The Christ

Colour: **Clear/Red**

Keynotes: Light and inspiration enters the physical world

Where to apply: Around the circumference of the body over the lower abdominal area. (Should not be used too late in the evening, because it may be energising which could result in sleep difficulties).

Main points concerning this bottle: Someone who has come through suffering to find the new energy within. Bringing into the light the energy that lies within. Reveals the potential and accepting who you are, yet with a sense of detachment or watchfulness.

Specialities of this bottle: The sixth bottle in the Aura-Soma Master Sequence. Could be of assistance if one wishes to awaken the Kundalini force. May support the process of coping with possible abuse. May relate to the test that is indicative of whether or not someone is able to take on spiritual responsibility. It would be helpful to look at B11 which is the intense version of this bottle.

Issues that may need to be addressed: The need to recognise the anger, frustration and resentment that lies within and to let go of these feelings through allowing the emotional release necessary (which could result in tears). Not to seek revenge in circumstances in which one may feel re-active.

Pale Violet/Pale Violet

Colour:
Keynotes: The walk along the pathways of the Highest order

St. Germain

Where to apply:	Around the hairline.
Main points concerning this bottle:	When we let go of the past we are more able to get in touch with our true spirituality. This combination suggests someone who has entered that process. A loving and peaceful person. A sensitive thinker, an inspirational teacher and healer.
Specialities of this bottle:	The seventh bottle in the Aura-Soma Master Sequence. Helps to bring male and female aspects together. May help people who have had a religious experience to integrate it into ordinary life. This bottle relates very much to the energy of Jupiter. Everything that applies to B16 also applies to this bottle in a more intense form.
Issues that may need to be addressed:	Someone who may be immersed in negative thoughts and cannot release themselves from these. A need to look at why we do not accept ourselves; to discover where we need to make changes.

B57

Pallas Athena and Aeolus

Colour: **Pale Pink/Pale Blue**

Keynotes: Let go and trust, personal independence

Where to apply: Around the body in the lower abdominal area, around the throat, and along the hairline.

Main points concerning this bottle: Main points concerning this bottle: A peaceful person who accepts themselves. They are aware of their limitations and potential to overcome obstacles. Someone who understands the Laws of the material side of life in a wholesome way.

Specialities of this bottle: The eighth bottle in the Aura-Soma Master Sequence. It may help to relate to experiences in Ancient Egypt and Ancient Greece. May help to bring conscious recall to those interested in dream work. Everything that applies to B29 also applies to this bottle in a more intense form.

Issues that may need to be addressed: It might be necessary to look at how the right side of the body manipulates the left, and through this means, address the male-female balance within. A need to accept the self - who you are and not hold on to one's anger. May be narrow-minded or have fanatical beliefs. May be pre-occupied unnecessarily with issues of survival.

B58

Orion and Angelica

Colour: **Pale Blue/Pale Pink**

Keynotes: Mother love, father love, spiritual love

Where to apply: Around the circumference of the body in the abdominal area, the throat, and around the hairline.

Main points concerning this bottle: Here we find a catalyst with the potential to be able to give love. Someone who is sensitive and balanced. A person who has a love of peace; whose faith can build bridges between mind and matter.

Specialities of this bottle: The ninth bottle in the Aura-Soma Master Sequence. This Bottle is an intense version of Bottle B20 (Blue/Pink) Star Child. Everything that applies to that bottle also applies to this one in a more intense form. Useful for travellers.

Issues that may need to be addressed: Someone who is being held back by not letting go of thought patterns. In connection with family issues - healing the parental situation, rivalry amongst the children, or not wanting to be part of a family situation. A need to accept oneself.

B59
Lady Portia

Colour: **Pale Yellow/Pale Pink**

Keynotes: The potential for great joy and happiness

Where to apply:	Around the circumference of the body over the entire abdominal area.
Main points concerning this bottle:	Someone who is able to accept who they are without fear of judgement, their knowledge has come because they have found love. A balanced and harmonious person. The knowledge and joy that has been deep within is now brought out in the context of self-acceptance. Caring and warmth for the benefit of everyone, because this is someone who realises their interdependence.
Specialities of this bottle:	The tenth bottle in the Aura-Soma Master Sequence. Has been used in the context of re-birthing. May be helpful for someone who has been dealing with interdependency/ co-dependency issues. The notes of this bottle should also be read in the context of the notes of B22, this being a more intense version.
Issues that may need to be addressed:	Someone who, because of their fears, needs to look at survival issues. To consider all the possibilities within a situation, rather than judging themselves when they miss so much.

B60

Lao Tsu and Kwan Yin

Colour:	**Blue/Clear**
Keynotes:	Be still and "know" who you are

Where to apply: Around the entire throat and neck.

Main points concerning this bottle: Someone with a clarity with which to express their feelings. They have come to peace in relation to that which has caused suffering. The peaceful communication in the mind gives the possibility of the release of tears and then to share what's seen with others. The light within gives the ability to see things as they are.

Specialities of this bottle: The eleventh bottle in the Aura-Soma Master Sequence. Can act as an "in-between" combination and precursor for other Aura-Soma oils (see "Specialities of this Bottle" for B11). The only Master Bottle that varies in colour from its corresponding Quintessence.

Issues that may need to be addressed: Someone who holds on to their emotions, particularly sadness and does not allow themselves to express their feelings. A need to be honest with oneself and so find joy and happiness.

B61 Sanat Kumara and Lady Venus Kumara

Colour: **Pale Pink/Pale Yellow**

Keynotes: As Above so Below

Where to apply: Around the circumference of the body in the abdominal area.

Main points concerning this bottle: Someone who has deep joy and happiness; warmth and caring not only for themselves but also for others. Someone who has realised their interdependence upon all things/people.

Specialities of this bottle: The twelfth bottle in the Aura-Soma Master Sequence. This combination may be useful to establish contact with the mystical traditions in Ancient Egypt, Ancient Greece and the times long before. This combination relates to the energy of Venus (regarding abuse see "Specialities of this Bottle" of Bottle B5). It would also be useful to refer to the notes for Bottle B40 as this is its most intense form.

Issues that may need to be addressed: Fears and anxieties of being alone. Feelings of abandonment. The sense of loss in relation to one's parental models. Having reached up from deep inside, a contact with the Kumaras may have been formed.

Pale Turquoise/Pale Turquoise

B62

Maha Chohan

Colour:
Keynotes: The sea of pure Universal Consciousness

Where to apply:	Around the circumference of the body in the chest area and around the entire throat/neck.
Main points concerning this bottle:	Someone with outstanding creative ability who is able to help others through listening to their problems and understanding their needs. A humble person, who may be involved in media or computer technology.
Specialities of this bottle:	The thirteenth bottle in the Aura-Soma Master Sequence. Relates to the Uranus principle. See also the notes for B43 as this combination relates to all the points made there but in a more intense form.
Issues that may need to be addressed:	Over-sensitivity or those easily shocked. Someone who does not easily let go of past heartbreaks, or the fears from the past. They may also be holding on to confusion and suffering because of this.

B63

Djwal Khul and Hilarion

Colour: Emerald Green/Pale Green

Keynotes: New beginnings brings balance and justice

Where to apply: Around the circumference of the body in the chest area.

Main points concerning this bottle: A person who has the courage to speak their truth. A person who has a capacity to integrate great feelings and is able to perceive the emotions of others. Has great perseverance and determination, knows where they are going and how to get there.

Specialities of this bottle: The fourteenth bottle in the Aura-Soma Master Sequence. This combination may help to establish contact with issues of persecution (for example, the Inquisition) and can help to release the trauma that resulted. This is the only bottle in the Master Sequence without a direct correspondence to a quintessence though both Djwal Khul and Hilarion have their own. Vicky Wall said "The reason that two Masters appear in this combination has to do with humanity's journey at this point in time between the Solar Plexus and the Emerald of the heart.

Issues that may need to be addressed: A need to give space and take the time to feel what is required when there are decisions to be made. Dwells on the negative side of issues instead of looking for the positive. May be incredibly confused. Lacking in joy and peace.

B64

Djwal Khul

Colour: **Emerald Green/Clear**

Keynotes: I am the way.... listen and follow

Where to apply: Around the circumference of the body in the chest area.

Main points concerning this bottle: Someone who has clarity of mind to seek the true self within. There is the potential to release that which has been lying upon the heart. A clear channel between thought and action. New beginnings, particularly in relation to one's mission and purpose. The search.

Specialities of this bottle: The fifteenth bottle in the Aura-Soma Master Sequence. Useful for people who are especially searching for the hidden patterns in life - like astrologers or those looking for a deeper understanding of colour.

Issues that may need to be addressed: A need to face emotional disappointment and fear. Let go of past anxieties and that which is not peaceful. The need to release the confusion around emotional situations and to see clearly why one has suffered.

B65

Head in Heaven and Feet on Earth

Colour:	**Violet/Red**
Keynotes:	The "I Am" comes to Earth Transformation

Where to apply: Around the circumference of the body in the lower abdominal area; and along the hairline.

Main points concerning this bottle: Someone who contemplates before putting energy into action. An intuitive and spiritual person who can guide others to their spirituality. Helps with the transformation of the self physically, emotionally and spiritually.

Specialities of this bottle: May show whether one might be putting energy towards people or situations where they could get abused or lost. Useful in guiding frequent sexual fantasies into a direction where the passion that is in the background can express itself differently and more constructively. (B6 is hidden in this bottle; also B60 so both of these notes could be taken into account in relation to this combination).

Issues that may need to be addressed: May feel threatened by those in authority and have a lot of hidden anger which erupts quickly when roused. If anger is released then there is a real potential for watchfulness and real awakening. There cannot be real progress here until one releases the anger, frustration and resentment.

Pale Violet/Pale Pink

Colour:
Keynotes: Unconditional love in the service of others

B66 The Actress

Where to apply: Around the circumference of the body in the abdominal area; and along the hairline.

Main points concerning this bottle: Someone with the potential for unconditional love and compassion which they express in relation to others. A balance between the physical and spiritual. Transformation can take place in the mind through the love, warmth and caring that lies within. A peaceful person with detachment within themselves.

Specialities of this bottle: Brings actors in contact with the essence of the parts they have to play. Shakespeare said "All the world's a stage and all the men and women merely players: they have their exits and their entrances; and one man in his time plays many parts." This combination can help us understand the tensions we hold. See also notes for B65 as this combination relates to all the points made there but in a more intense form.

Issues that may need to be addressed: Someone who may have experienced extreme difficulties with parents during childhood. May let others down by ignoring their duties. Not to expect from others unless you're prepared for the consequences which may be by being too easily disappointed. Someone who finds it difficult to commit to relationship and is therefore always frustrated because of superficiality in contact with others, even those cared for. Not being able to discriminate between when one is or is not acting.

B67

Divine Love, Love in the Little Things

Colour: **Magenta/Magenta**

Keynotes: Love Divine merged into service

Where to apply:	Everywhere on the body (also excellent for use as a body oil).
Main points concerning this bottle:	Someone who is loyal and reliable; who will go beyond the call of duty. A creative, compassionate person; selfless in relationship. Someone who has a lot of love to give to others, to animals and the planet - gives love to all the little things including the inanimate.
Specialities of this bottle:	All Chakras may be able to function better. Useful in rebirthing, and also in other therapies, when a higher level has been attained and something new is about to begin. Generally supportive when a new chapter in life begins.
Issues that may need to be addressed:	Someone who overworks and finds it difficult to have time to themselves. Someone who is looking to receive from others the quality of love similar to that which they readily give. Subject to many disappointments.

Colour: # Blue/Violet
Keynotes: Peace and fulfilment, spiritual discernment

Gabriel

Where to apply: Around the throat/neck; and along the hairline.

Main points concerning this bottle: Someone who is able to communicate their spirituality and intuition. The healing is communicated to others through their work in the world as a social worker, speech therapist or spiritual teacher. An idealist bringing ideas to the fore. A peaceful person with a lot of energy to get things done.

Specialities of this bottle: If the bottle appears in the third position, it may mean that something new and unexpected lies ahead. That a new clarity is about to come and things can be seen more clearly in the future. This combination could help us to grow in the context of relationships and to see them as opportunities for our own growth.

Issues that may need to be addressed: Someone who may speak without thinking; may have difficulties with the father figure or may idealise this role too much. A person who appears on the surface to be brave but inside harbours deep resentment or frustration.

Sounding Bell

Colour:	**Magenta/Clear**
Keynotes:	Purified desires, love's energetic drive

Where to apply: Everywhere on the body (excellent as a body oil).

Main points concerning this bottle: A charismatic person whose light shines from within radiating love and compassion. A creative person who puts the love which comes through them in all the little things. Someone who finds joy within the family situation.

Specialities of this bottle: A bottle which could help us to focus on what is in front of us. To move beyond ideals to practicalities. To know we have the support of "Love from Above".

Issues that may need to be addressed: Someone, not having found love, may be holding back the tears. May be bored with life and, as a result, take unnecessary risks (either emotional or financial). A person who may feel empty inside not recognising how they are suffering.

B70
Vision of Splendour

Colour: **Yellow/Clear**

Keynotes: Let's shine the Light into the Astral fog.

Where to apply: Around the circumference of the body in the whole Solar Plexus area.

Main points concerning this bottle: Someone by looking at the self discovers a clarity of mind and thus eliminates confusion. Knowledgeable, someone who finds joy through insight into the nature of suffering.

Specialities of this bottle: Can facilitate "automatic writing". May help to experience integration of phenomena that have been difficult. To find the joy in the unusual.

Issues that may need to be addressed: Fears and anxieties prevent enjoying all that life and living can offer. Not allowing others to experience the gifts that they have been given as a person. It is our fears that make us suffer the most.

B71

II. Essene-Bottle
The Jewel in the Lotus

Colour:	**Pink/Clear**
Keynotes:	Lift in consciousness through limitless power of love

Where to apply: Around the circumference of the body in the lower abdominal area. Additionally, a drop may be applied to the top of the head.

Main points concerning this bottle: Someone with love, care and warmth for others, who has a clear insight to see the love and warmth they have, and the love and warmth which they need to give to themselves - true self-acceptance. A watchful person with the power of compassion.

Specialities of this bottle: This combination may connect with Essene incarnations. May be helpful with cranio-sacral work to release the cranial plates.

Issues that may need to be addressed: Someone who may be holding back the tears due to not tending to their own needs. A person who feels unloved or has a feeling of not being recognised. Denies the love that they know they have and so denies what lies deep within. A lack of recognition in relation to anger and resentment which, here, are the causes of suffering.

Colour:	**Blue/Orange**
Keynotes:	The communication and nurturing of inner emotional desires

B72

The Clown
(Pagliacci)

Where to apply:	Around the entire trunk.
Main points concerning this bottle:	Someone who, from their own experience, is able to help others with insight and understanding. Communicate the essence of bliss to everyone. Persevere as the efforts of your labour will eventually come to fruition.
Specialities of this bottle:	This combination is said to change cellular structure and thus may be helpful in possible hereditary diseases and genetically acquired illnesses. Helps attain harmony with one's own instincts. (Blue/Orange are complementary opposites. A Bottle with many deep implications).
Issues that may need to be addressed:	Difficulty in communicating following a deep shock. A need to overcome dependency/co-dependency and fear from the past to find the peace. No sense of humour - a need to be able to laugh at yourself or at the circumstances that life presents us with.

B73 Chang Tsu

Colour: **Gold/Clear**

Keynotes: Wisdom from the depth of the self

Where to apply: Around the circumference of the body over the area of the belly.

Main points concerning this bottle: Someone who is aware of the wisdom they carry and has the inner clarity to put it to good use. May be going through a purification, a process of a lightening inside.

Specialities of this bottle: May be of help when someone is not assimilating properly. This can be information, impressions or food. Can help to integrate experience.

Issues that may need to be addressed: Egotism, engrandisement, self-glorification. Someone who is jealous or envious of others. A person who has become materialistic and forgotten the treasures buried within.

B74

Triumph

Colour: **Pale Yellow/Pale Green**

Keynotes: Justice through balance

Where to apply:
Around the circumference of the body in the heart and Solar Plexus areas.

Main points concerning this bottle:
Someone who is true to themselves and has a sense of joy in their heart. To express those feelings from the heart to others. To be harmonious and balanced. Someone who has made the space for themselves to become clear in relation to their intellect.

Specialities of this bottle:
This bottle has much to do with the emotions. For example, at the beginning of a new relationship it may be useful to clarify the feelings. Is especially useful for varicose conditions.

Issues that may need to be addressed:
Anxieties and deep fears. Fears of having no feelings or emotions. Things don't flow as they should because of not trusting what one feels.

Go With the Flow

Colour: **Magenta/Turquoise**

Keynotes: A change of view. An opportunity to see things differently

Where to apply: Everywhere on the body.

Main points concerning this bottle: A warm and loving person who can communicate from their heart. Someone who may help others to view things differently, from a different angle or to deal with things from a new perspective. A person who is committed to the process of Individuation.

Specialities of this bottle: The contents of this combination may help to release energy when it has built up anywhere in the system and become blocked. Facilitates the ability to "go with the flow" again. We can only look back from where we are now. If we had come to a different point then the past would also appear different.

Issues that may need to be addressed: A need to love and so let go of negative thoughts or hurts from the past. Hidden fears need to be realised and anger translated to discipline in relation to a new way.

B76
Trust

Colour: **Pink/Gold**

Keynotes: Wisdom of the past expressed through unconditional love

Where to apply: Around the circumference of the body in the area of the abdomen.

Main points concerning this bottle: A watchful person, detached, centred and compassionate, very joyous. Someone everyone enjoys being with. One who is loving and caring; is able to find the wisdom that lies within.

Specialities of this bottle: It is possible that this person belongs to a group concerned with the development of man. May be able to help the individual enter previous lives more easily. Supports rebirthing. Can relate to someone who finds it difficult to remember the past, possibly because it is too painful.

Issues that may need to be addressed: A need to let go of confusion, fear and anxiety from deep within to allow care and attention for the self to come in. It may be that this person finds if difficult to allow others to see the gifts/talents they possess. Intense frustration can prevent us from getting in touch with the wisdom that lies within.

B77
The Cup

Colour:	**Clear/Magenta**
Keynotes:	Love and light manifests, physical perfection

Where to apply:	Everywhere on the body.
Main points concerning this bottle:	Someone who has clarity of mind and knows the deep love they have to put in all the little things. A clear channel for the love from above to be enjoyed by the self and distributed through one to others.
Specialities of this bottle:	May connect with Essene incarnations (see Bottle B11 and also The Christ Bottle B55).
Issues that may need to be addressed:	A need to focus the attention in one location and not to try to cope with too much at once. One knows how one has suffered and it's now time to release this in the context of love.

Crown Rescue

Colour: **Violet/Deep Magenta**

Keynotes: Peace loving and dependable

Where to apply: Around the hairline, also around the throat and neck, the Third Eye, and the crown of the head.

Main points concerning this bottle: Someone who puts their attention into the little things not only for the self but also in the service they offer to the world. A spiritual person. Also, someone who is true to themselves. A person who's in the middle of a psychological transformation. A spiritualisation of self.

Specialities of this bottle: This bottle was the first to be born after Vicky Wall's death. It is also called the "Divine Rescue". In psychotherapy, this combination helps to bring light to the past, thereby creating success in the present. Relates to the Pleiades, the "Great Bear", and Canopis Major. This combination can be helpful to those who want to work with Devas, Angels, and the unseen.

Issues that may need to be addressed: Someone who has a false sense of security; may have made an inappropriate choice. A possessive person, even holding on to grief when it could have been let go of long ago.

B79
The Ostrich Bottle

Colour: **Orange/Violet**

Keynotes: A deep healing from within for a shock situation

Where to apply:	Along the hairline and around the circumference of the body in the abdominal area.
Main points concerning this bottle:	A spiritual person with insight. Someone who heals those suffering in shock situations, may have suffered a shock themselves and are healing from deep within. There may be a desire to find deeper insight, to find the spiritual within the self or one's service in the world.
Specialities of this bottle:	Can point out that someone is confronted by their own death or the death of a friend or relative. An indication of intense change. May help break free from addictions. May connect with incarnations in Ancient Egypt.
Issues that may need to be addressed:	Someone suffering from a shock that may be preventing healing taking place or allowing their spirituality to emerge from within. A person not identifying with who they are due to not releasing the blockages within. Someone who is hiding from who they are and denying themselves deep joy.

B80
Artemis

Colour:	**Red/Pink**
Keynotes:	Energy to love and release, a letting go bottle

Where to apply: Around the circumference of the body in the abdominal area.

Main points concerning this bottle: Someone who has unconditional love, warmth and caring and the energy to bring these forth - an awakening - to share with others. To be able to balance the "inner" self with the "outer" self.

Specialities of this bottle: People who work in caring professions can, with the help of this combination, reconnect with their resources of love and their physical strength when they are depleted. Hidden within this bottle is B2 (Blue/Blue) and B42 (Yellow/Yellow); the two other primary colours - the yellow sun shining on the blue of the earth brings forth the red energy for life.

Issues that may need to be addressed: Allowing the material side of life to dominate rather than finding a balance. Anger and resentment caused by not feeling loved, or love being repressed or rejected.

B81

Unconditional love

Colour:	**Pink/Pink**
Keynotes:	Compassionate and understanding the need for love

Where to apply: Around the circumference of the body in the abdominal area.

Main points concerning this bottle: Someone who is sensitive and caring; needs to give love to others; and is able to nurture themselves. A watchful person who is very present to the circumstances of life.

Specialities of this bottle: Supports the rebirthing process and sessions. Clears patterns relating to persecution that occurred in former lives. May help to develop intuition.

Issues that may need to be addressed: There is a need to feel wanted. Don't forget to give yourself love. Beware of too much pride. There may have been a problem as a child between yourself and your mother which needs to be examined.

Calypso

Colour: **Green/Orange**

Keynotes: The space to connect with the insight from within, deep bliss from the heart

Where to apply: Around the entire trunk.

Main points concerning this bottle: Someone who is able to open their feelings and their hearts to share the wisdom they have with others. They are wanting to express the love in their hearts with great joy. Has gut reactions and deep insights. This person has a real sense of freedom.

Specialities of this bottle: This combination may help to retrace emotions. As a result, useful insights can be gained as to why one feels the way one does.

Issues that may need to be addressed: A need to let go of any conflicts, shocks or traumas from the past. Dealing with any anxieties that lie deep within. The difficulties experienced with the male authority figure now need to be let go of.

B83
Open Sesame

Colour: **Turquoise/Gold**

Keynotes: Heartfelt communications of the wisdom of the past

Where to apply:	Around the entire trunk.
Main points concerning this bottle:	A person who has an inner wisdom and can communicate it with feeling to others. Someone who prefers to share with a group rather than on a one-to-one basis. Has a love of the mineral kingdom, who has profound wisdom within. An understanding of the new technologies.
Specialities of this bottle:	May relate to incarnations in Lemuria, Atlantis, Ancient Egypt, with the Aztecs and Incas, as well as with the mystical traditions of Europe. May bring a connection with crystals and an opening to the Devas that work with them. Hidden in this bottle is B4 and so the issues contained therein also apply, as does the B8.
Issues that may need to be addressed:	Fears and anxieties which restrict communication or expressing oneself. A lack of confidence or feeling a lack of self worth.

B84 Candle in the Wind

Colour: **Pink/Red**

Keynotes: Compassion for the passion within, the desire to care

Where to apply: Around the circumference of the body over the abdominal area.

Main points concerning this bottle: Someone who has the energy and passion to give unconditional love. Has awakened to one's female intuition, through self-acceptance and has the discipline necessary to change the patterns of the past.

Specialities of this bottle: The combination supports tantric work, which means the transformation of sexual energies into spiritual energy. (This doesn't imply sexual practices). For more information see B6 which also pertains to this bottle; Pink being a more intense version of Red.

Issues that may need to be addressed: May have frustrations in relation to acknowledging the love they need or could give. May have resentments in connection with their femininity or in relation to the mother model where love is not returned in the way it is given.

B85
Titania

Colour: **Turquoise/Clear**

Keynotes: New Age communications, inner illumination

Where to apply:	Around the circumference of the body in the chest area.
Main points concerning this bottle:	Someone who is charismatic and communicates the Light with feeling. Someone whose learning takes place in the context of teaching. Also, likes new technology to keep in touch with others through the internet or e-mail. Not a lateral thinker but someone with joy in creative input.
Specialities of this bottle:	May aid those who have (had) problems with implants. May be able to help release creative blocks and bring in a new light.
Issues that may need to be addressed:	Someone who has been unable to shed their tears as their feelings are trapped inside. May not be able to express themselves creatively. May have difficulty with the masculine side of the self because of the suffering created by holding on to hidden fears.

Clear/Turquoise

Oberon

Colour:
Keynotes: A channel for the creative communication of the heart, the light media communications

Where to apply: Along the hairline or around the circumference of the body over the chest area.

Main points concerning this bottle: Someone who has clarity of mind and is able to bring their feelings from their heart and communicate them to others. To be able to balance one's positive and negative energies. Has a lot of creative depth which is presented in a lightful way.

Issues that may need to be addressed: Difficulties in communicating feelings from within because of intense suffering. May need to be more assertive in communications which could come through letting go of hidden fears.

Love Wisdom

Colour:	**Coral/Coral**
Keynotes:	The wisdom at all levels, unrequited love. Interdependence

Where to apply: Around the circumference of the body over the lower abdomen, as well as along the right side of the body, from the right earlobe down to the right ankle. The opposite side from B26

Main points concerning this bottle: The potential to give love and wisdom to the world. Someone who accepts themselves, who is involved in "waking up". They have an understanding of inter dependence, which has brought them deep joy.

Specialities of this bottle: May be helpful therapy when dealing with the subjects of shock, abuse, and unrequited love in past, as well as present, incarnations. May establish a connection with past lives spent in the North American Indian tradition.

This also applies to B26 and B54. See notes on B26 as Coral is more intense version of Orange. The information on Orange is relevant to understand the Coral.

Issues that may need to be addressed: A feeling that one's love is not being returned. Someone who may have difficulties with relationships from the past. Someone who may have suffered some form of abuse in present life or previously.

Jade Emperor

Colour: **Green/Blue**

Keynotes: The communication of peace through feeling

Where to apply: Around the circumference of the body in the chest area; and over the entire throat and neck.

Main points concerning this bottle: The feelings of spaciousness allow you to find some peace and harmony within. Someone who has found peace within themselves is now able to communicate their feelings. A nature lover, an ecologist, a worker for reform in consciousness of Gaia.

Specialities of this bottle: Assists people who feel that they do not belong on Earth. May connect with incarnations in Atlantis, Lemuria and with the Knights Templar. For helping us get in touch with our feelings, when we don't make space to allow that process to take place.

Issues that may need to be addressed: Someone who may have difficulties with their masculinity. There may be a fear in connection with authority. They experience difficulty in expression of their emotions, feelings or the truth. If peace could be found then there may be an intense joy to be lived.

B89
Energy Rescue

Colour: Red/Deep Magenta
Keynotes: The Time Shift

Where to apply: Around the circumference of the body in the lower abdominal area.

Main points concerning this bottle: Someone who is looking at the shadow within themselves to find the energy to awaken their transformation. A person who has the energy to bring their healing instincts from within. Intuitive and spiritual and has an extraordinary relationship and understanding of time.

Specialities of this bottle: This bottle was born on July 26, 1992, when the calendar of the Mayans showed the end of a cycle. Therefore, this bottle is also called the "Time Shift Bottle". Is suitable for tantric exercises. Helps people who work with Earth energies. May protect from negative Earth energy radiation.

Issues that may need to be addressed: Someone who does not wish to utilise the energy they have and to decline the opportunities that life presents to them. A need to address the feelings of anger, frustration and resentment. One of the chief problems could be in attention to detail.

B90
Wisdom Rescue

Colour: **Gold/Deep Magenta**

Keynotes: A deep healing in relation to the Ancient Wisdom

Where to apply: Around the circumference of the body in the area of the abdomen.

Main points concerning this bottle: Someone who has found the love and compassion within themselves. Is able to put the love into the little things and so discover immense joy and wisdom through what they have to share with others.

Specialities of this bottle: Aids people who have condemned themselves so much for their little mistakes that they cannot express their strengths. May connect people to incarnations with the Mayans, Aztecs or Toltecs.

Issues that may need to be addressed: Not being able to let go of deep fears and anxieties to find the love within. Confusions in the mind and frustration because of not recognising the depth of love within.

B91
Feminine Leadership

Colour: **Olive Green/Olive Green**

Keynotes: The lessons of the heart

Where to apply: Around the circumference of the body in the chest and abdominal areas.

Main points concerning this bottle: Someone who is a leader, with passion expressed from the heart who trusts their feminine intuition. Has the ability to understand scientific and spiritual matters and explain to others, so that they may also understand. Is a very truthful person with qualities of integrity.

Specialities of this bottle: People who are under the impression that they are aggravated by extra-terrestrials will find clarity in their situation by using this combination. Helps to come into the right relationship with the unknown. Also see B2 and B42.

Issues that may need to be addressed: Fear - the fear of feminine power, to look at the feminine side of the self and the fear of authority. Relationships which, emotionally, are not suitable, creating the same "mistakes" or patterns in relationship over and over.

B92

Gretel
(as in Hansel and Gretel)

Colour: Coral/Olive Green

Keynotes: Independence of the feminine, co-operation not competition

Where to apply: Around the circumference of the body over the belly and chest areas.

Main points concerning this bottle: Someone who is going through personal change and personal growth and has found love and wisdom with which to quell their fears. Through their love they may be able to help others who are fearful, and then to be able to develop trust and hope for the future.

Specialities of this bottle: Hidden in this bottle is "Pallas Athena and Aeolus" (B57 Pale Pink/Pale Blue). The energy of this combination also has a lot to do with the energy of Zeus/Jupiter. It supports the work with the "inner child". It is also helpful in difficulties relating to finding our "right livelihood". Bottles B92 and B93 were born almost at the same time. They have been named Gretel and Hansel, respectively, because the Hansel and Gretel fairy tale demonstrates an aspect of these bottles very well: they stand for the female aspect of the "inner child" (Gretel) who trusts in her intuition and overcomes her fear, pushing the witch into the oven; and the male aspect of the "inner child" (Hansel) who places his trust in the female aspect. He is therefore released to find true joy and happiness.

Issues that may need to be addressed: To be in difficult situations through being negative. A need to address the conflicts within oneself. The need to trust the process of life.

B93

Hansel
(as in Hansel and Gretel)

Colour:	**Coral/Turquoise**
Keynotes:	Collective communication of love wisdom

Where to apply: Around the entire trunk. "Humans not elephants".

Main points concerning this bottle: Helps with self-examination to find the trust to communicate with one's feelings. Someone with loving attention and wisdom to transform the negative to positive. An ability to communicate to many as well as to individuals.

Specialities of this bottle: See notes of Bottle B92. This bottle can also be of assistance in letting go.

Issues that may need to be addressed: To see what you are looking at and not what you imagine it to be. Someone who needs to face the issues of being dependant upon others.

B94
The Archangel Michael

Colour: **Pale Blue/Pale Yellow**

Keynotes: The Higher Will meets the little Will

Where to apply: Around the circumference of the body over the heart and/or navel areas and also the throat.

Main points concerning this bottle: Someone who has found peace is now able to let go of the confusion within. The joy that we have within is released when we let go of the fear. A time of great change when many familiar things fall away to reveal something new.

Specialities of this bottle: This bottle is the first of the Archangel sequence. It is the more intense version of B8. Please examine the comments upon this bottle and imagine a more intense situation.

Issues that may need to be addressed: Someone who has a fear of authority, through not allowing the peace to be released from the confusion. The need to balance the emotions; to let go of jealousy and envy and the feelings of wanting to be where someone else is or wanting what someone else has.

B95

The Archangel Gabriel

Colour: **Magenta/Gold**

Keynotes: Love from above fills the star

Where to apply: One drop on the top of the head and all around the area directly below the navel.

Main points concerning this bottle: Someone who has Divine love and the inner wisdom to understand the meaning of such love; who puts the love into the little things. All actions are performed with care and warmth. A person who is undergoing a great change in their life, a new beginning combination.

Specialities of this bottle: The second in the Archangel sequence. This bottle contains the Red/Gold, the "I Am" Bottle, perhaps reading the notes for this combination would also be helpful.

Issues that may need to be addressed: A person suffering from deep fears or confusion. A need to be true to oneself and not to fall into old habits or patterns. There could be much hidden anger or frustration in this combination. It is this energy which makes it an awakening bottle.

Royal Blue/Royal Blue

B96

The Archangel Raphael

Colour:
Keynotes: The Higher mind functions, nurturing

Where to apply: Along the entire hairline, on the brow and on the feet.

Main points concerning this bottle: Someone who has found deep peace which they then give to others. A person who can keep focused and not be distracted by comments of others. Has found clarity in seeing, hearing and feeling. Trust yourself as you become more detached more inner peace develops.

Specialities of this bottle: The third in the Archangel sequence. May help with clarifying the senses. A little rubbed over the forehead could help seeing, hearing, trusting, smelling and even touching.

Issues that may need to be addressed: A need for discipline, and a letting go of anger, frustration and resentment so that it does not hold you back. The need to allow the creativity that comes to you to express itself.

B97

The Archangel Uriel

Colour: Gold/Royal Blue

Keynotes: The Incarnational Star links to the Higher mind functions

Where to apply: Along the entire hairline, on the brow and temples, around the heart and Solar Plexus area.

Main points concerning this bottle: The potential to be in contact with your feelings; the feelings you have for others and the communication of these. A person that has a deep peace within which is beginning to come to the surface. Someone who has a heart of gold. Someone who has found enthusiasm for life and is in touch with their centre.

Specialities of this bottle: The fourth in the Archangel sequence. This combination shakes together as the Emerald Green which is where we might get in touch with our service and purpose in the world.

Issues that may need to be addressed: A need to examine our values. Someone who needs to remain humble. Deep anxieties need to be let go so as to connect with the inspirational qualities that are being fed in from above.

B98

The Archangel Sandalphon
Margaret's Bottle

Colour: **(Pale Violet)Lilac/Coral**

Keynotes: Transmutation of negativity on all levels

Where to apply: Over the top of the crown or lower abdomen.

Main points concerning this bottle: Someone who has joy, bliss and insight within them which is now beginning to be visible to others. A person that is in the process of change and has the gift of unconditional love to help them through this. The Higher Will assists them in communication with Devas and Angels.

Specialities of this bottle: The fifth in the Archangel sequence. It may be helpful with cranio-sacral work. To help the cebro-spinal fluid to flow more easily. In this work it could be applied over the whole length of the spinal column.

Issues that may need to be addressed: Someone who needs to deal with the issues of abuse they may have suffered in the past. Allow healing of unrequited love to take place. If one is always a catalyst for change then it is easy to lose oneself.

B99

The Archangel Tzadkiel
Cosmic Rabbits

Colour: **Pale Olive Green/Pink**

Keynotes: A step into the waters of life

Where to apply: Just above the Solar Plexus in a band around the body. Also, over the base of the spine and around the pelvic girdle.

Main points concerning this bottle: This combination opens the possibility for light to be shone upon the feminine intuition. For you to allow the feminine in ourselves to be supported by unconditional love, unconditional self-acceptance. Someone who has these qualities is a pioneer for freedom. A secret agent for truth.

Specialities of this bottle: The sixth in the Archangel sequence. May be useful in helping us to get in touch with who we really are; to access our true purpose and mission.

Issues that may need to be addressed: It is now time to let go of the fears, to accept what lies within. To realise that the anger, frustrations and resentments are holding one back and to use this energy for awakening.

Colour: **Clear/Deep Magenta**
Keynotes: Light in the darkness illuminating the Shadow

Metatron

Where to apply: Can be applied anywhere on the body, particularly helpful over the back of the head and neck and around the temple line. Can also be applied as in Reflexology (on the soles of the feet).

Main points concerning this bottle: To help with inner relationships, to help us to see what is most difficult to see. There are certain things that block our awareness within ourselves. Metatron is there to bring awareness to those obstacles. It represents somebody who has suffered, is aware of the type and reason for the suffering and how there is now an opportunity to release that, to let it go at the deepest level. For those who put on a brave face.

Specialities of this bottle: It belongs to the Archangelic series within Aura-Soma. Metatron is defined as the King of the Angels and also the Angel of Covenant. He joins Heaven and Earth together. It is part of the capabilities to put us back in touch with a real sense of our Being.

Issues that may need to be addressed: If it is difficult to face what lies within the shadow, if it is difficult to see the truth of ourselves, to come to an understanding of the forces within our own unconsciousness then this bottle may be of help to bring light to all of this.

Pomanders and Quintessences

POMANDERS

The pomanders work within the electro-magnetic field surrounding the physical body. Each pomander can help to introduce the energies of colour to which it relates, to help bring into our experience the positive messages of that colour. They are essentially protective – cleansing, refreshing and strengthening to the energy field. Kirlian photography has shown that they create little valves within the electro-magnetic field that allow the positive energies in and filter out energies that are less helpful. They can also be used as a means to focus our intent. They support that part of us at the centre which is at ease.

Pomanders contain the energies of colour, herbs and crystal. They are a combination of forty-nine herbal extracts and essential oils. Within each pomander there are seven different herbs related through their colour to each of the seven chakras, forty-nine herbs in all. Each pomander will contain a predominance of the herbs that correspond to the particular chakra to which the colour relates. The forty-nine herbs are always present in each pomander even though the proportion of each herb will change according to the colour. Within the white pomander, the forty-nine herbs present are in equal balance, 7 x 7. Each of the pomanders addresses the needs of a different chakra and brings certain qualities of energy to it depending on its colour.

TO APPLY: Place three drops in the left hand. Rub the hands together. Extend the arms above the head giving the energies away to the world. Distribute gently through the energy field beginning at the crown and working your way down the body making sure you cross every chakra point. Rest for awhile over the heart chakra before continuing on through the solar plexus, hara and base chakra and then offering the energies to the earth. Imagine or visualise the energies of the pomander penetrating deep into the layers of the earth. Then bring the hands up, palms together in front of the face and take three deep breaths into the body. Use daily to cleanse the electro-magnetic field and to strengthen and support the aura.

Included in this book is a description of each of the pomanders, the qualities that they introduce into the electro-magnetic field, and the support that they bring to the whole being.

WHITE
Keynote: Brings in light and renews; brings clear perception.

This is the original pomander with the combination of the 7 x 7.i.e. all forty-nine herbs in equal balance. Cleansing, purifying and protecting, it may be used in any space to cleanse atmospheres, bring the light in and renew energies. Helpful during detoxification. It protects all chakras and the whole of the electro-magnetic field. As it contains all forty-nine herbs in equal balance it brings balance to the chakras. It's very good for clearing/cleansing quartz crystal. It is harmonious and harmonic with quartz and can therefore help programme a quartz crystal or clear old programmes. May be used in water and sprinkled to freshen a room. As the negative energy gathers around a person during a situation to pressure its identity, the white brings the light down to this situation.

PINK
Keynote: Warmth and caring, to love ourselves.

The Pink pomander surrounds us in a loving atmosphere helping us to bring out the best in ourselves. It brings emotional wellbeing by bringing in love, caring and warmth. Pink represents the basic ground within which we all function, the warmth and caring which makes everything possible. It is a specific for harmonising group energies and for neutralising aggression. Protects when somebody has opened up for love/true love. Surrounds us in a loving atmosphere helping us to bring out the best in ourselves. It is harmonious with and amplifies and supports the energies of rose quartz.

DEEP RED
Keynote: Grounding, protection from earth energies, the most re-energising.

Works with harmonising the base chakra and is helpful for grounding after meditation or any therapy session. Provides the strongest protection for energy zapping, being energising and restoring physical energies after tiredness and fatigue or from depletion through drugs. De-stresses the electro-magnetic field. Helps with all kinds of fears linked to survival issues – money, health etc. Activates the right half of the brain and brings in deep feminine intuition. Warming and energising, it can also have an aphrodisiac effect. Can be used in house clearing by neutralising psychic activity and help to protect during rituals and sacred dances. Sacred sites and power places have very often been used in an incorrect manner therefore it is recommended to protect yourself from these energies with deep red pomander. Protects people that work with gems. Helps to balance electro-magnetic polarities in the body. Deep Red also protects against geopathic stress, negative ley lines and psoric water and helps to restore the polarities that have been upset by any of these.

RED
Keynote: Grounding of purpose, everyday protection, re-vitalising.

Everything said about the Deep Red also applies to Red. Red is more for the everyday situation whereas deep red is for extreme situations. Red stimulates the hormonal system bringing back energy in a very gentle way in cases of tiredness. Helps to overcome disappointment and shyness. Helpful for grounding after meditation or any therapy session. Both Reds de-stress the electro-magnetic field.

CORAL
Keynote: To learn how to love and care in a new way.

Helps us to learn how to love and care in a new way. An awakening energy. Healing of the unrequited love issues, especially of the self. For loving the parts of us that are most difficult to love and feeling how those parts of ourselves respond. Helpful with the acceptance of our responsibilities with a sense of joy rather than hardship. For loving our fears, helping us to move closer to synchronicity. The healing of the *time line. Also helpful for altitude sickness.

*A time line is the continuity of consciousness from its beginning to its end. Each shock or event is a point or wave on this line. A distortion due to all kinds of patterns of interference can move the emphasis on the time line that in turn reduces synchronicity. It is possible through the integration of these events or shocks that more synchronicity can be resumed. This also applies to the Orange pomander.

The Coral is applied on the right side of the body not the left as the Orange.

ORANGE
Keynote: Regression and shock absorption, bringing insight.

The Orange relates through the etheric body. Between electro-magnetic field and the astral body is the etheric body. It is through the etheric body – to which the body relates – that past and future experiences may be accessed. Using the Orange pomander allows the informational content of past experience to be accessed, without bringing emotionally cathartic aspects into the present. This opens the door to insight.

The etheric gap is at the bottom of the left rib. It is an escape chamber used in big traumas when the aura moves out through the gap. The Orange pomander is a regulator for temperature i.e. if aura feels warm/cool work on etheric body. Good for all shock situations. *The healing of the time line.

A specific that can help with bedwetting and for those prone to nightmares. Good for the parent to share with the child as the Orange relates to co-dependency.

Brings a more relaxed point of view to people who encounter difficulties with technical appliances. The

Orange pomander is helpful as a regression protector and far memory shock absorber of the past. In regression work use St. Germain first, then the Orange pomander. This protects the user and opens the door for knowledge from the past. Applying this substance helps to let go of the negative effects of experiencing past trauma.

GOLD
Keynote: Release from irrational fear, reconnecting with innate wisdom.

Gold helps us reconnect with our instinct. Assists researching your wisdom as a being. The Gold allays irrational fears and phobias, and can heal peer group difficulties, connecting each to the confidence of self within. The Gold assists in breaking the habitual and emotional patterns, addressing the fears that lie behind these patterns be they mental, emotional or physical. The Gold can bring wisdom for the individual to realise what is leading to the pattern therefore can be helpful if somebody wants to overcome one's addictions by helping to access this deeper wisdom within oneself. Helpful with extreme anxieties in exam situations. Helps with the assimilation of food and energy. Helps in overcoming deep irrational fears and assists in easing tensions in the solar plexus. Connects us to the Incarnational Star.

YELLOW
Keynote: Antidote to nervousness and negative thoughts, brings back the sparkle.

Sunlight, Self Knowledge, Assimilation. The Yellow can help to allay nervousness and anxiety. Yellow brings the sunshine in and acts as an antidote to the blues so is useful in cases of depression or where there is a lack of sunlight (SAD – Season Affected Disorder. The pineal is the 'light governor' of the body and reacts in response to darkness by regulating the control of melatonin. Lack of sunlight has the effect of 'shutting down' the body, as if preparing for a hibernation stage.) Also useful for jetlag for the same reason.

Yellow is for accessing knowledge. Specific for patterns of addiction and helpful in detoxification. (Also see Gold). Yellow is critical in assimilating the energies of food and water. We are nourished not only by food and water but the entire energy field of the environment received as Prana, principally through the solar plexus. The pomander feeds the wavelengths of herbs and gems to restore and regenerate that area and bring balance within.

If anyone is negative bring in the Yellow. For those in a depressive state Yellow unlocks joy. Helps with sickness and travel sickness and if you have a repulsion against something. Helps with mental nervousness and anxiety. Stimulates intuitive knowledge.

OLIVE GREEN
Keynote: Cleansing and refreshing our space.

Both the Green pomanders invite the feeling-being response, so are useful for emotional issues. They go to the heart of things.

Olive helps to overcome anxieties, fears and disappointments that have to do with feelings. Encourages feminine leadership from the heart – cooperation not competition, and enhances the ability to stand up for one's truth. Recommended when somebody is at a crossroads or in processes of decision.

It is anti-pollutant and disinfectant. In the subtle bodies it is useful for clearing jealousy, envy and other negative emotions. Helps with all issues of space, both agoraphobia and claustrophobia. Recommended for therapist's use between sessions, helping to step out of one space and into another by clearing the space between clients.

The Olive is feminine intuition, a knowing that arises out of the caring for something. The fear of giving space is that we may be overwhelmed by shadows or what is hidden. The Olive Green assists in enabling the space to come into balance so as not to manipulate or control that which is arising.
A quality of feminine wisdom is compassion. With nervous fear, it brings wisdom into the heart and releases the fear, helping us to find our own way.

EMERALD GREEN
Keynote: Finding our own space, going to the heart of things.

Calming, balancing and centring bringing peace to the emotions. Always an anti–pollutant, a disinfector, Emerald Green is wonderful for the heart chakra, opening and calming the heart, helping to expand the breathing.

Supports all heart concepts – connects with the truth of the heart. In close situations, difficulties with other people and confrontational situations, Emerald Green brings clarity of communication in one's feelings. Provides the space to find our own way and free ourselves of old ideas. This helps with decision–making for those at the crossroads of life. Helpful with all issues of space, both agoraphobia and claustrophobia. Can bring a deep link with nature, especially trees. Creates the feeling for space and the feeling that the space is protected and respected. This is very helpful for therapists and consultants to keep the distance between client and consultant. Enhances decision-making processes and brings new direction. Supports any breath work. Brings peace into our space. An antidote for those who are 'spaced out.' As with inoculations when a little of the bug is given to protect, a little Green pomander can be more effective antidote to spacing out than using the Red.

Both Green pomanders link time and space so support memory by helping us locate where we have filed the events of time, helping us to remember. Anti-pollutant and disinfectant for both the environment and the subtle bodies.

For those who are beginning to seek/search, the use of the Green pomander can lead to a new beginning, new awareness, a new consciousness. Emerald Green allays fear by bringing peace into our own space. For balance and encounters with the shift into the 4th dimension.

TURQUOISE

Keynote: Creative communication of the heart from the feeling side of our being.

The Aquarian Pomander, facilitates the communication of New Age wisdom. Turquoise releases creativity, encourages communication from the heart and keeps inspirational communication flowing. E.g.: radio, T.V., stage talks.

For all creative pursuits – writing, painting, dancing, massage etc. Opens up for one's own creativity to come through. Helps with stage fright and technophobia. Helpful in cases when somebody doesn't know what they feel. Assists counselling. Helps us to express what lies in our feelings, to express from the heart. Protects the communication of love and caring, taking some of the vulnerability from it. It encourages independence and the ability to take responsibility for our feelings and actions.

Recommended for people that work in the mass media. It enhances communication with crystals and Devas and facilitates our rapport with computers and silica technology. To connect in a creative way with the collective archetypal world in the mental body.

SAPPHIRE BLUE

Keynote: Communication that comes through us and to lift us from suffering.

The Blue pomanders support the highest communication of love, fostering the inspirational and devotional aspects. They help us find the Spirit within the worldly. Deepens the peace within us. As we become more peaceful, we become more clear, we expend less energy in our own pre-occupations and therefore have more energy available to do what it is that we need to do. Supportive in meditation, protecting and bringing peace. Brings inspiration and trust within inner guidance. Helpful for particularly sensitive people. Useful for those who experience difficulties with authority and with people in authority. The journey backward and forward from death to life – transition is made through the Blue energy so the Blue pomander is particularly helpful during the transition phase. For those suffering from terminal illness, bringing calm, peace and tranquillity.

Both the Sapphire and the Royal Blue will bring peace to the transition or help to bring the energy to support the person's return to life. They are helpful for those working with death and dying or for those in rebirthing or midwifery. Blue represents the Mother of us all as well as the Father

The Blue pomanders bring us into alignment with the Divine plan, providing protection for the communication that comes through us rather than from us.

Helpful in accommodating role reversals in families, where Fathers have the responsibility for nurturing the children and/or where Mothers are the breadwinners by choice. The Sapphire relates to the pure Blue and the throat and provides support for those who speak publicly or teach groups. For a hyperactive child, may bring calm, peace and tranquillity.

ROYAL BLUE
Keynote: Inner peace, inner seeing.

The Royal Blue relates to the brow and third eye and fosters the development of the higher mind functions, e.g.: clairvoyance, telepathy etc.. Provides protection for channelling. The higher the communication the more the need for protection. The more light generated , the more the dark will be interested. For people that like to build castles in the air, utopianism, it brings them back to the ground.

Helpful with deep depressions. Amplifies the perception of all the senses, enhancing the pleasure and enjoyment that comes from listening to music.

Opens to imagination and intuition. For those with difficulties in relationships, it helps them relate. For those also working with sound – chanting, mantras, toning etc. Helps you to go beyond, to be sensitive, to go over the bridge.

*NOTE: Both the Blue pomanders have a strong peppermint content and care should be taken not to neutralise homeopathic treatments if used in combination.

VIOLET
Keynote: Calming and healing; beautiful before meditation.

The Sweetness of Spirit – Vicky Wall's favourite.

The Violet pomander opens perception and awareness of the higher realms, helping us to connect with our mission and purpose. Helps with seeing what one can do to serve others or life in general. The access to Akashic Records.

Good for calming all situations and over energy in the head. Helps balance the electrical flow between the two hemispheres of the brain. Supports the process of relaxation in a dynamic rather than a merely passive sense and is a beautiful pomander to use before meditation, to go deeper. To support the transformative process. For the making whole circumstance.

To make contact with the other side. The bridge between grief. Helps to overcome grief after loss and to find new direction and eventually to see the sense behind it all. Once information has been received, helps with assimilation helping thought processes to come through. Helps to go beyond limitations on all levels and gives access to new experiences. Opens for the miracles that are hidden in the everyday.

DEEP MAGENTA
Keynote: Energised compassion, deep caring.

The Carer's Carer. For those who have given all their energy to others and now need to receive caring for themselves. Provides all the energy we need in a gentle way, bringing the love from above into the auric field. Leads to self knowledge and finding out about one's task and purpose in life. Helps create the golden moments. Combining the Red and Violet energies, the Magenta pomander is both energising and soothing at the same time. Helps to keep focused. To keep investing in the right account within ourselves, putting caring into the little things so that the big events take care of themselves. Helpful when a nuclear family breaks up. Brings the energy to clear up or bring order to the little things in one's life that tend to be put aside for more important things. Helps to do everyday little things with love/caring.

Harmonises intellect and instinct. Opens for quality of consciousness and understanding on all levels. Helps to build up energy after depression and is very protective. Helps to 'tune in' to nature. Makes it easier to get access to a deep meditative state. Can be of support if somebody has to cope with a very difficult experience.

The most helpful pomander to stabilise treatments that work on particular reflexes or energy points, such as acupuncture and reflexology. To seal the energies at the end of a session, apply a couple of drops to the points worked to help energies go on a little bit longer.

QUINTESSENCES

The Quintessences bring a more subtle energy into the Aura-Soma colour system. They work through the astral and etheric levels to facilitate the flow of energy from the inner planes. Their function is invocative. When we use a quintessence we invite into the auric field the most positive energies of the colour rays to which they are related. As we do this we are invoking our own qualities into manifestation from deep within us. The Quintessences help us to accept and recognise our own inner beauty.

The Quintessences relate to the Master range within the Equilibrium set. These are the bottles from B50 to B64 inclusive. Each Master vibration brings with it certain qualities, certain experiences. We can use the Quintessences when we are willing to open to bringing these experiences into our life.

The Quintessences can be used to help you with meditation, prayer, contemplation, taking you to a still place, connecting you with the Source of Universal energy.

TO APPLY: Place three drops on the left wrist and gently rub the wrists together. Extend the arms above the head, giving the energies away to the world. Then gently bring the hands in and cross the wrists over the crown. Continue to open and close your arms in this manner as you come down and cross over each of the energy centres, stopping to rest over the heart chakra for a few moments. Then continue down and give the energies to the earth. Then spinning the hands in a backward spiral, bring the hands all the way up the front of the body before once again giving the energies to the world. Finally, bring the palms together at the forehead and deeply inhale the quintessence three times into the body.

Included in this book is a description of each of the quintessences, the qualities that they invoke into the auric field, and the support that they bring to the whole being.

EL MORYA – Pale Blue

Keynote: "Thy Will be done through me".

The main purpose of this quintessence is to increase communication through the astral and etheric bodies to invoke peace. I Will that thy Will be done through me from heaven to earth. Helps you come to that point within yourself to let the Divine Will be done. Brings abundant energy – by becoming more peaceful, energy is released. It calms the subtle bodies and brings peace, making information accessible to the consciousness which is in the astral body. Inspires creative communication, stimulates creative abilities. Helpful to those who have had Mother/Father problems from the beginning. Also for those having difficulty finding the role models within themselves. Helps people to find clarity in situations with their parents. Helps bring about the nurturing of the Mother and the wisdom of the Father. El Morya stimulates the feeling of being at one with all things. It is an antidote to the negative sense of loneliness: all one rather than alone. To bring about more grace and ease.

This quintessence brings a strengthening of the Will and enables one to align oneself with one's purpose. For Quintessence recommendation, aligns with Blue.

KUTHUMI – Pale Yellow

Keynote: Love – Wisdom; nurturing the Angelic-Human-Devic communication.

"Come to me" – an invocation to the positive energies of the future. Points towards enlightened self-knowledge. Relates to the Maitreya Buddha who looks after the future.

One of the main functions of Kuthumi is to help humans find their role between the Angelic and the Devic kingdoms in order that we may receive an understanding of the Divine plan through our intuition from the angelic realms that ground it upon the earth. This is a role exemplified by St Francis, one of the principal associations to the Kuthumi energy.

The communications of the Angelic kingdom through the human kingdom to the Devic kingdom (mineral and plants, elements such as fire, water, air and earth). Devas belong to the earth - we humans act as a link to the Angels for the Devas. At this present time the Devas are in chaos due to the lack of caring from humans. Kuthumi helps with attunement to plants - links with Devas, Angels and fairies. Supports people that wish to contact the beings like Devas, plant spirits or Angels for healing work, gardening or in meditation.

Amplifies and deepens the ability to see through processes and to understand backgrounds and connections – how things are linked.

Kuthumi helps make the connection to your familiars

- these are personal symbols - often animals in nature e.g. a witches' black cat, an eagle or a unicorn. Opens for the energy of animals. Brings luck into one's life by bringing in the positive qualities. Kuthumi also opens us to an understanding of science and number and relates to Pythagoras. Invokes those energies within the Auric sphere to give a different understanding of forms and energies.

This quintessence brings in Wisdom and Unconditional Love. For Quintessence recommendation, aligns with Yellow.

LADY NADA – Pale Pink
Keynote: Unconditional Love.

Relates to the sixth energy centre, the third eye, two petals. A quintessence to improve our capacity to relate. (Nada in Sanskrit means sacred sound - the inner sound – Om). Lady Nada helps us to be heard.

Healing with deep love. Letting go of negativity at a deep level. As the negative aspects of the personality are digested by the spark of Divinity within, this allows us to experience a kinder response from the Universe since our thoughts about ourselves create our reality. Whatever you experience is only what you deserve by what you think of yourself.

Brings in the pure love of the Divine Mother. Brings a personal experience of truth within ourselves. Truth becoming the Living Truth, then Divine Wisdom comes from the acceptance of that.

This is the most anti-aggressive of all Aura-Soma substances - it changes negative energies into positive energies on all levels of life. Clears the auric atmosphere and environment of negative vibrational states, bringing in the higher aspect of love that we may become nurtured. Helpful for clearing aggression from the auric sphere. Protects the user and therefore changes the behaviour of the aggressor. Brings back the flow in communication that has been blocked or is threatening to get stuck.

Connects to the Moon which takes the negative energy from earth. Helps people that are affected by the rhythm of the moon in a negative way. Enhances full moon meditations.

For those working with sound, links with music and voice and to help the integration of light within ourselves. Brings an understanding of the way light and sound intermingle within the auric sphere.

This quintessence clears the aura of negative emotions by the transmutation of negative energy into positive energy – bringing in the highest vibration of unconditional love. For Quintessence recommendation, aligns with Royal Blue and Pink.

HILARION – Pale Green
Keynote: A space for the new.

The Way, The Truth, The Light.

The Way:	as we come to know ourselves better, our direction becomes more clear.
The Truth:	the expression of ourselves.
The Light:	as our consciousness raises, we become more light-filled.

Helps to create space within oneself, to get to know oneself better. Allows the user to find the peace and space for decisions. Hilarion makes a space for the new and helps to release old identifications that are no longer useful, affording us an opportunity to step into the present anew. In the middle of stress, this quintessence can bring stillness, peace and space for decisions.

A new direction and a new space. Hilarion is the key to unlock the door. Expression of truth, clarity of direction.

Brings access to one's own wisdom and truth and helps us to understand things that have been understood with the head to be understood with feelings as well so a true integration becomes possible.

The higher feeling aspect of the heart. Space and new beginnings. The peace to find the wisdom of truth, the feeling connection with understanding. If we are prepared to let go of all that we have in the past, then we can come to a new space and a new understanding.

Clears environmental pollutants. Refreshes the parts other Quintessences don't reach. This quintessence helps protect against earthly pollution and clears one of inner or outer deception, refreshing the soul with truth. For Quintessence recommendation, aligns with Emerald Green.

SERAPIS BEY - Clear
Keynote: Purification and new beginnings.

Karmic Absolution – seeing karma in a new light, as an opportunity for healing rather than as a burden.
Serapis Bey - releases you from karmic seeds of the past by Absolution of the bodies. Light shone on past experience brings you illuminated to the present.

Can help to expand the vital aura, balance the aura, seal and protect it. Expansive to and amplifies the electro-magnetic field, links to the stars and attunement to stellar energy and the Goddess Sophia (Truth and Wisdom from above).

Cleanses the room at the end of a therapy session and helps the therapist to clear their own space. Useful at the end of a session - to protect, harmonise and seal the aura. Helps the client to integrate their experience more easily.

Especially useful for work with quartz crystals which are looked on as being keys for the access to the mineral kingdom. Helps to access the inner dimensions of crystals. Can be used for energetic cleansing of crystals.

Begin something new. Absolve yourself from the past. Shine the light on a subject, maybe it isn't what you thought. There is no need for Karmic suffering - Absolve yourself with Serapis Bey. To be used at the start of any project. Good for detoxifying on all levels. Stimulating of Mudra, sacred gestures - particularly of the hands, and balancing.

This quintessence gives a depth of understanding into conflict, pain and suffering on any level.

For Quintessence recommendation, aligns with Clear.

THE CHRIST – Red

Keynote: Re-energising, deep protection and caring.

The Deep Red of The Christ brings in sacrificial love with a new degree of caring, a new degree of loving. If we shine the light through it, it becomes pink – the unconditional love. The consort of The Christ is Lady Nada who brings through the highest vibration of unconditional love. We can each have a personal experience of The Christ by however much we allow the consciousness to touch us. Brings an understanding of one's own purpose in life and clarifies their relationship to the earth.

The Logos. The Word made flesh. To help a person connect with their spiritual purpose, where the light comes to earth. Christ is the awakened I AM. The truth expresses itself through you, the word made flesh. Supports people that have to talk and write a lot (logos). Brings them into contact with what it really is that they want to communicate.

Enables the user to approach an energy field that has to do with The Christ Consciousness/Bhudda field – a fully conscious illuminated person. This level can be reached or touched by any person whether Christian, Bhuddist, Hindu, member of a tribal religion, spiritually independent or even for the non-religious. Helps us to take responsibility for ourselves. We make inner connections with the Source through ourselves

Kundalini energy springs from the base and moves up through the crown. This quintessence is useful for those working in polarity therapy.

Brings rememberances of Christmas energies and smells, cedars of Lebanon, ancient embalming fluids.

This quintessence can bring a personal experience of The Christ energy into the auric sphere. The inbringer of the emancipation of womankind, balancing the duality of male and female principles within us all.

For Quintessence recommendation, aligns with Red.

ST GERMAIN – Pale Violet
Keynote: Healing, Meditation, Transformation.

St. Germain is a catalyst and transforms negative energies into positive ones. It invokes the higher energies, bringing wellbeing to all major energy centres and profound balance to the male/female balance within the self. To calm down the etheric, astral and electro-magnetic fields. To touch mind upon mind. Transmutation of energy to help to overcome issues to do with survival e.g.: money, security, health etc. To purify any base issues. It is very good for hands-on work as it helps us to detach and step outside of ourselves, allowing the energies to simply come through us. It is when we are most impartial and step outside of self; becoming detached and not too involved; that the best then comes through. Clears emotional problems that haven't been dealt with. Changes the energetic state e.g.: if someone is over-active/anxious/overstimulated – changes this kind of energy into spiritual energy.

To bring forth all the actors on the stage of life. Allows energies coming from the future to permeate the present. Helps to respond rather than re-act. Brings the keys to higher knowledge.

The Lilac Flame Of Transmutation. Transformation of Self. Facilitates the expression of you as a catalyst and transformer. Whatever the situation, you can transform and heal it. Helps new breath coming into the body. If the breath isn't fully let go of, we never know real gut level. Breathe out properly, allow new life to come in fully by breathing out and letting go. Relative to how much we let go of, is how much we are reborn in the now.

Vibrates with the keynotes of the French revolution: Liberty, Equality, Fraternity.
Amethyst as a gem returns things to their natural state.
This quintessence assists in re-birthing or regression sessions.
For Quintessence recommendation, aligns with Violet.

PALLAS ATHENA – Pale Magenta
Keynote: Creative expression of love and beauty.

The love of, and awakening to, beauty. Communication of higher truth. Revealing that which is normally hidden. What is hidden needs to be revealed and released. Brings heaven and earth into the grasp of all.

To become an active dreamer. Also leads to effective dreams. Gives access to inspiration and rememberances of the content of dreams, bringing insight into one's own dream symbolism, helping to decode dreams.

Supports while working with the overcoming of old patterns. Simplifies access to shamanistic traditions especially in the case where one wants to become familiar with the relationship to earth of the old people, Ancient Wisdoms. Relates to North American Indian traditions and particularly to the Aboriginal Song of the Earth. Brings a connection with the Greek and

Roman mythological world of the Gods. Revelations from the temples of the Gods and Goddesses of Ancient Greece. To amplify and enhance energies of rose quartz. To help with making our dream life more conscious.

Pink shines the light into the material affairs of the world. Helps us to be in harmony with the world through right livelihood. Right livelihood comes from following our true path. For those who dream dreams, see visions or create – through pen, paint, music etc. Encourages prosperity consciousness, in the sense that we have what we need.

Practise the energy – by using the appropriate energy in the small things in life then the quality will be there in the big things. We have a choice of what we practice. If we don't like the results in our life then we should change the practice. The attitude and caring we give to the little things will be with us when we need it in the big things.

This quintessence brings Heaven and Earth, bringing all within the grasp of us all.
For Quintessence recommendation, aligns with Magenta.

ORION AND ANGELICA – Pink

Keynote: For fresh beginnings, endings, and for journeys.

The two great Angels that open and close each day. Orion brings the sacred blue of space, Angelica, the sacred pink of cosmic love. As Orion brings in the night and draws the sun across the sky, (Orion's belt can then be seen in the night sky) so Angelica brings in the dawn. Angelica gathers all the impurities, clearing negativity at a very deep level, that which we no longer need, in and on, both us and the Earth.

Helps to tune into synchronicity. To be in the right time and the right place. Helps with the beginning and ending of projects. Brings light into the astral body, so supports methods which intrude into the subtle bodies. A dislike of the smell of this quintessence can indicate a difficulty in taking responsibility for the light that we carry. Useful for people interested in Earth healing and geopathic stress.

This quintessence is a journeying energy. It is the specific for jet lag as it aligns all the subtle bodies. Useful for travellers, especially air travellers. Apply Orion and Angelica for jet lag, for all the bodies to arrive on the tarmac at the same time. Apply to the wrists before take off, at the crossing of each time zone and after landing.

For Quintessence recommendation, aligns with Pink.

LADY PORTIA – Gold

Keynote: "Judge not" .. including ourselves; seeing clearly brings right action.

Judge not lest ye be judged. For those who are hard on themselves. Self-judgemental/critical. Being merciful with ourselves is true compassion. The harder we are on ourselves the more we bring criticism from others. Whoever has a tendency to criticise or judge others can learn to develop compassion. On the other hand it also becomes conscious that true perfection can only happen if one is able to see oneself, others and specific situations in a critical manner. When self criticism is indicated application of Lady Portia can help to develop a feeling of how this can be done in an appropriate and polite manner. Mercy/Love with true clarity are exemplified through this quintessence. The mercy with ourselves has to be turned in on ourselves which leads to true compassion.

Helps to express thought in a clear form, especially when linked to old wisdom and self recognition.
Brings discernment.

Combining Yellow and Pink - discriminative wisdom. Intense rebirth. Helpful for letting go. Relinquishing control. Helps with rebirthing therapy. Helps to overcome one's birth trauma and to let go of fear. People who are always working and never have a break. To help overcome fears in conscious mind. To help to formulate clear thoughts. Brings justice, balance and discrimination. Seeing a situation clearly in order to know the right course of action.

Helps to eliminate negative vibrations. Clears the environment quickly. Brings in the light quickly.
Connects with the Solar Plexus - the central sun of our being.

This quintessence brings back balance when one is not centred: discriminative wisdom.
For Quintessence recommendation aligns with Gold and Yellow.

LAO TSU AND KWAN YIN – Pale Orange

Keynote: Release from the past, bringing in compassion.

Lao Tsu was a Master Alchemist of the past and now brings in the ability to transmute and transform energies.

Facilitates regression - particularly for clearing deep regression shock. To help bring information from past lives towards you. To help to transmute energy of past situations - alchemical transmutation. Brings understanding and appreciation for what it is that we have experienced in past times and helps us to grow in self-acceptance. After this it allows for a feeling of deep peace. Helps to receive information from earlier incarnations without having to deal too much with the shocks that may be related to them.

Helps us understand what lies behind dis-ease. Undo the problem and find the gift. It often lies within the attitude. Use the technique to change the attitude and thinking and you change the patterns of life. It works on patterns of tensions at a deep level - releasing tensions in the body-mind, assisting the functions of the energy centres. To bring in peace, compassion and deep nurturing.

Helps to overcome shocks related to sexuality. Helps with the kind of shock where a teenager/child has given their best at school but the teacher will not recognise that. In this case Lao Tsu & Kwan Yin can be very helpful – same for adults in similar situations.

This quintessence brings the Healing Ray flowing in Mercy and Compassion of the Father-Mother God and releasing the oldest memories of the ancient Chinese wisdom.

For Quintessence recommendation, aligns with Orange.

SANAT KUMARA AND LADY VENUS KUMARA – Pale Coral

Keynote: Bringing the Divine into everyday, seeing to the depths of things.

The Mother and Father principles at the highest level. Sanat Kumara and Lady Venus Kumara are responsible for the in-flowing of all the rays to the world at this time. They operate on the law, "As Above, So Below." What is going on in us is going on in the Divine, the Angelic kingdom and the Source as well as also below in the plant, mineral and animal kingdom.

When in doubt use this quintessence. As administrators of all the rays they help to access any ray. Helps us to get to the bottom of things, to find out what lies behind a particular issue. When there's been abuse or difficulties in the past it helps to bring about a positive connection to the female/male role models within the self. On another level it makes a bridge between this side and the other side so is useful to people working on bridge building between the spirit world and our own, particularly in this time frame. Very useful for deep emotional shocks.

The secret of the Universe is within us. This quintessence helps us to make the link to the deepest aspects within ourselves, to that spark of Divinity. The more conscious we become, the more we can participate in the Divine process.

Brings in a new octave, a step up to a higher level of vibrations.
A dislike for the smell can indicate difficulties in letting go, especially of emotional issues.
This quintessence brings special awareness of Divine Life into the everyday.

For Quintessence recommendation, aligns with Coral.

MAHA CHOHAN – Pale Turquoise

Keynote: Bringing to awareness what we need to say, from the feeling side.

The Greater Teacher. The only Master not to have incarnated. The Teacher of the other Masters.
Lord of Civilisation for Lemuria.

Teaching through the whisperings of the heart. Helpful in releasing feelings that need to be expressed.
Helps to make contact to inner teacher/inner master.

Enhances inspiration of people who work in mass media or who express themselves through improvisation with music and dance or theatre. Helps also if someone is practising intuitive massage or if somebody has to speak without having time to prepare for it.

This quintessence can encourage the positive qualities of the Light Workers and the Rainbow Warriors. Helps to make a feeling connection both with oneself and others. Brings feeling through from the heart. Makes the feeling side of being more concrete. Makes one aware of the life of the feeling being.

Helps the expression of New Age Wisdom in all contexts. Brings one in touch with the Inner Teacher, one's personal link with the Master energy within the feeling side of one's being.

The link with the higher vibrational states to help the communication through the feelings with the Angelic realms. Brings a feeling of a personal relationship with the Angelic realms. A space to connect with the Master vibration.

This is the Aquamarine of the Age of Aquarius, the Atlantean resurgence, working in power for this period of time, long awaited, to bring in the Law of the New Civilisation of Light Conscious ascending souls.

Genetic Engineering and the potential misuse of power is in the memory banks of everyone. Animals and plants are being experimented on now as they were changed then. The linking between mind and spirit, resurrecting pre-scientific knowledge in its deepest aspect – i.e. it addresses the potential misuse of power, especially with genetic engineering from Lemurian times.

For Quintessence recommendation aligns with Turquoise.

DJWAL KHUL – Emerald Green

Keynote: Seeking the truth.

The most ardent of seekers, Djwal Khul is the seeker of Truth – not in the sense of Narcissus, but for the sake of Truth. Djwal Khul is D.K., the Tibetan in the writings of Alice Bailey, who helped usher in the new psychology.

The seeker for truth, in the sense of a search for objective truth beyond the subjective reflection of the seeker. The Seeker's Master for Truth and Purpose. To help us find the space within, the relationship between inner and outer space. To create balance and harmony within the subtle bodies, to stimulate the Green within the major chakras. Can be helpful to stimulate a balanced intuition. A cloak of emerald protection for the heart. As you clear your own space, you come to direction and truth within your own heart.

Brings an understanding of rhythms, laws and patterns of nature. Forwards an understanding of astrology and the esoteric.

Creates a balance within the subtle bodies. Grounds people that are opening up to their intuitive side. Also helps them not to be overpowered by the information gained through intuition. Especially helps people suffering from fears to open up to clarity and self-acceptance.

This quintessence is for those who intuitively know they occupy space beyond the Earth.

For Quintessence recommendation, aligns with Emerald Green.

HOLY GRAIL AND SOLAR LOGOS – Pale Olive Green

Keynote: Be receptive and listen carefully.

Designed to stimulate receptivity and openness and to be able to allow the communication to flow through us. The Pale Olive becomes a bridge from the solar plexus to the Emerald of the heart. It can help on all levels of being to bring about a transformation in relation to receptivity and unfoldment of the creative feminine intuition within each of us. It helps us to remember that whatever we seek lies within us.

For Quintessence recommendation, aligns with Olive Green and Pale Olive.

For further information please contact:
Aura-Soma Products Limited
South Road
Tetford
Lincolnshire
England LN9 6QB

Tel: +44 (0)1507 533581
Fax: +44 (0)1507 533412
E-mail: info@aura-soma.co.uk
www.aura-soma.net